Life's
FISHING
MANUAL

Life's FISHING MANUAL

Crucial Principles for Attaining Success We Don't Learn in School

Calvin Thean

PARTRIDGE
A Penguin Random House Company

Because of the dynamic nature of the Internet, any web addresses or links contained in this book may have changed since publication and may no longer be valid. The views expressed in this work are solely those of the author and do not necessarily reflect the views of the publisher, and the publisher hereby disclaims any responsibility for them.

To order additional copies of this book, contact
Toll Free 800 101 2657 (Singapore)
Toll Free 1 800 81 7340 (Malaysia)
orders.singapore@partridgepublishing.com

www.partridgepublishing.com/singapore

Contents

To my wife, Dorothy,
who has been the constant inspiration
of my journey to self-discovery,
and my sons,
Timothy & Zachary

Introduction

Give a man a fish, as the saying goes, and you feed him for a day. But teach him to fish, and he will be fed for life.

The adage reveals the distinction between helping someone by alleviating a temporal plight and helping through empowerment. Help the man by feeding him, and you are merely addressing an immediate problem. But very soon the problem will return. The man becomes hungry again. But give the man the intangible gift of skill and knowledge, and if he is prepared to accept and apply this gift, he will never go hungry again.

In the same way, we frequently help one another in times of need: a temporary setback, an emotional breakdown, financial difficulty, and so forth. We think nothing of it, as the desire to help a fellow human being come naturally. Commendable as these efforts may be, we are merely addressing the symptoms to the underlying issues. Without the skills to help overcome these life situations or to avoid them in the first place, very soon we will find that the person is "hungry" again and in need of help.

I am of the view that we all, whether consciously or unconsciously, seek the core principles that would help us create a fruitful, purpose-filled life that is rich with wonderful and happy experiences. Formal education provides us with academic subjects such as mathematics and science, arts and humanities, languages and such. But beyond these foundational knowledge, we are left to discover these core principles for ourselves. Perhaps it's better that we each discover the principles in our individual ways, so that each of us can craft a life experience that is uniquely ours. Yet it certainly wouldn't hurt to have some guidance to point us in the right direction.

Consider the following situations and see if any of them are familiar. You may have experienced one or more of these situations yourself or it may have happened (or is happening) to someone you know:

- have you ever taken stock of life and asked yourself "Is this it?", "Is this all there is to life!?";
- you are convinced you have the necessary commitment, drive and motivation to succeed in whatever you choose to do. You just need someone to tell you which way to go. Because of the lack of direction, you are working hard, proverbially spinning your wheels, and not going anywhere in life;
- you are frustrated because deep down inside, you are convinced that you are meant to do much more in life. You know that you are capable of fantastic things, if only the right people and the right breaks come your way;
- you are frightened that life has passed you by. You realise you're not getting any closer to your dreams. You are essentially stuck in a dreary dull routine-filled life. You are doing the same job, always going to the same places, meeting the same friends, eating the same food, talking about the same subjects, worrying over the same issues, and doing the same pastimes on the weekends;
- you have, from time to time, achieved some significant successes in life. But you are frustrated because you're not being able to find a process to consistently achieve the desired results and success at work, and in your personal life;
- you feel as if you're existing in a dream-like state (or living nightmare may be a more apt description). At times you catch brief tantalising glimpses of your true capabilities. Yet you're unable to truly break free of this dream-like

existence to reach your life goals. It's as if you are being held back limitations, both real and imagined. And you feel the frustration and hopelessness of the situation;

- you've just started out in life, and are curious to know if there is, amongst all the myriad information and books out there, a "system" that will give you a head-start in life; or

- you seen other people whom you define as "successful" and said "I wish I could be like them.", "They're so lucky.", "Luck (or success, money or good things) comes to other people, but not me."

If any of the situations above resonate with you, and you are experiencing frustration, disappointment and a sense of hopelessness, I want to tell you that life can indeed be better. Much better. Trust that God and the Universe intends much better things for you. I believe that if we seek hard enough, we will eventually find that we are looking for. But we need to have the right mental attitude, and to take the appropriate action and in the right direction.

I don't know at what stage you are in your personal development, or what were the circumstances by which you came across this book. However it was not by pure chance that our life paths have crossed in this way, and I am glad for this opportunity. This book is my way sharing the principles that I hope will help you navigate through life and point you in the direction where you can start achieving your aspirations and life goals.

What this book can do for you will depend on how much you're prepared to commit in time and effort to put the principles and skills into practice in your daily life. All knowledge is pure potentiality until it is put into practice. Learning anything without putting it into practice is merely transferring the knowledge from one "vessel" (a book or a teacher) to another (the reader or the student).

What this book won't do is:

- tell you what you should do with your life;
- tell you what the meaning of life is for you;
- give you a fast, easy and effortless shortcut to your dreams and goals; or
- give you a secret "one solution to all problems".

Quite the opposite, applying what is suggested in this book requires awareness, plenty of effort, persistence, and discipline. You will need to continuously assess your progress, adapt what you are doing and constantly seek to improve. Last but not least, you will also need humility and a great desire to learn.

While it is possible to achieve success in *any* aspect of life, it's necessary to have one common understanding up-front. There are no short-cuts to success. Nor are there are any "instant success" formulas. A meaningful and successful life is unlike cooking instant noodles. Lasting meaningful results will not come about quickly, requiring just minimal effort on your part. Lasting change and success demands an investment of both time and effort. It is the price that must be paid to reach each and every one of your life goals.

The ideal situation

If we all had our way, the ideal situation is one where we achieve our life goals without ever leaving our comfort zone. We attain our goals effortlessly, whilst maintaining our current comfortable lifestyle. Unfortunately this is not possible. If you are **not** already achieving your life goal living your life the way you are doing now, it's very likely that you will need to change what you are doing in your life, or the way you are doing things.

> Depending on how far away your "trajectory" is towards the desired goal, the changes may be uncomfortable and require a substantial amount of changes and adjustments. For instance, the goal concerns your health, this may mean a change in diet, your eating habits, starting an exercise regime, and even having less leisure time or waking up earlier to accommodate the exercise regime This may indirectly impact your daily routines as well as how you allocate your time and energy on your other activities.
>
> If it's to attain a certain educational qualification, it may mean enrolling and attending classes and studying during whatever free time you have. In the same way, the classes will impact your existing lifestyle and routines. It may mean having to make adjustments to your lifestyle to accommodate your studies.

This commitment is also the very thing that separates the people who are "achievers" from those who merely wish. It separates the truly deserving from those who passively dream of what could be.

The maxim "there are no short cuts in life" holds true even in nature. Consider this: the plant with one of the shortest known life span is the Arabidopsis (*Arabidopsis Thaliana*). It is a small flowering plant that is native to Europe and Asia. It has a life cycle of just six weeks, and it grows to no more than 25cm (10 inches) in height. At the other end of the spectrum of the plant world, one of the tallest trees known to man is the the giant redwood (*Sequoia sempervirens*). They are known to grow up to 115m (or 379 feet). However it takes the Sequoia up to 20 years to grow (just) 20 meters! In the same way, the amount of time and effort you're prepared to invest in pursuing your life goals will determine the scale of your achievements. You can decide whether you want to be just a short shrub, or the tallest tree in the forest.

Through this book, I hope to encourage you to firstly, start off on the path of reflection and self-discovery; secondly, encourage you to acquire more knowledge whether by reading or learning from other sources of information, and thirdly, putting whatever you've learnt into action and practice. For it is only by continuing to learn and practice that we continue to grow and potential to blossom.

I hope that certain parts of this book will reach out and touch you, and help you see things in a new and fresh perspective. To inspire you to reflect and begin a change from within. I also hope that this book will encourage you on to read more and explore the various topics covered in this book.

Some pointers to help you along

Before going further, there are a few personal insights that I would like to share with you. These are things that I have experienced myself whilst reading self-improvement books, and I hope that these insights will ease your passage through this book, as well as other self-improvement books.

Think

Reading self-improvement books is not a passive activity in the same way that you read a novel. To derive the full benefits of any self-improvement book, it's necessary to to take the time to reflect on the points raised. You may agree or disagree with what the author says. You are entitled to your own views. However what is important is that the book you read should prompt you to think about the ideas raised, and consider where you could make use of these ideas and suggestions to improve areas in your life. It's even better if the book causes new ideas and thoughts to spring up as you read it.

Relevance of the examples given

In this book, I will frequently use analogies to illustrate the points I'm trying to make as a picture (albeit a mental image) is worth a thousand written words. At times however, the examples cited may not strike a chord with you. For instance, the example used may involve the workplace, but you may still be studying and the example might not make any sense to you. Nevertheless don't disregard the message just because the example doesn't resonate with you. Although the physical context used may be alien, but the emotions and experience in the example are likely to be similar to those you have come across in other life situations that you may be familiar with.

This is a unique facet of life: although we each take a different path in life, however many of the situations we encounter during our respective life journeys engender similar emotions and experiences. The people, circumstances and environments may be different, but the emotions (joy, happiness, fear, frustration, anxiety, sadness, disappointment) and experience (the indecision, overcoming the inertia and fear associated with change, overcoming bad habits and attitudes, and the sense of accomplishment when we succeed) are likely to be similar to another person's or even those that we ourselves encounter in a different stage of life. Unless we learn and change how we address these situations, we will likely repeat the same mistakes. When you come across an example that may not resonate with you, pause and think of life situations where you may have come encountered these very same emotions and experiences. Be aware that there are skills and mindsets that can bring about an alternative outcome, so that in future when you encounter the same emotions and experience, you can put your newly acquired skills and mindset to use.

Words - they bear different meanings to different people

Words are merely tools that we use to communicate our feelings, thoughts and ideas to other fellow human beings. And they are very crude tools as they can never fully convey the full range of the intangible human emotions, feelings and experiences.

Several consequences flow from this. Firstly we must understand that although we may share some common basic understanding of what the words we use mean, yet a word may mean different things to different people. For example, the word "success" may mean raising children who are healthy, responsible and well-adjusted for one person, good health to another and achieving financial independence to yet another. Likewise the word "happiness" will also bring different mental images for different people. Therefore we have to understand the context in which a word is used when we are reading a book. Failing to do so may result in us not fully understanding the point the author is trying to make.

Secondly, we must be open to this idea that words may evoke different mental images, feelings and emotions for different people. Using the earlier example, since other people may have ideas of what happiness is that are different from ours, it does not mean that their opinion is wrong. There is no "right" or "wrong" view. We can only agree to disagree. Our understanding of different meanings and contexts that words may have will expand through experience. Hence re-reading books is important as the context of the material may become clearer once, over time, we have more knowledge and experience under our belt.

Words - they bear different meanings at different times

Words bring about different emotions and mental images at different stages of our lives. Hence it's important to understand what a particular word may mean to you now; and to use the suitable words to describe your life goals. Otherwise the goal, if described improperly, will fail to inspire us.

I will give an example. For myself, the word "humility" has undergone a great metamorphosis. When I was younger, humility meant denigration. Being in a position of being teased and humiliated. The word bore a negative connotation. And it caused anger rise up whenever I felt that the word was associated with myself or my status.

However through the years, the word now brings different associations. Humility now means looking beyond the self, and that I am just one human being amongst seven billion others living on a small planet which itself is a small speck in an infinite Universe. Viewed this way, all my self-centered worries and what I consider to be important are instantly put into perspective. Secondly, humility now means serving others and placing their interests above myself. Thirdly, it means being open to learning. Finally, humility is realising that all that I have, my achievements and experiences are not solely the results of my own efforts, but that each and every one of them are God's blessings.

So the mental images and emotions that words evoke will change as we journey through life. When describing yourself and your goals, choose words that convey images and emotions that are positive and empowering, and they will take you in the direction you want to go. Making the right choices also makes the journey all the more enjoyable, richer in experience and fun!

Re-reading materials

Once you have finished reading any self-improvement book, make it a habit to read it again after a period of time has passed. It is likely that you will find new ideas or information that had previously missed your attention. Passages that made no sense during the initial reading may now resonate with you. Or a passage in the book may convey one meaning when you first read it, but another at the subsequent reading. Or different words may touch you, and speak to you where previously they did not have much significance.

You may experience this more frequently when reading examples or analogies that are used to get the author's message across. After the first reading, the story may convey one message. But should you look at the story again months or even years later, you may see it differently. The picture remains the same, but the observer has changed. Where perhaps there was gloom and darkness, there is light. Where once you saw despair, you now see hope. Where once there was obstacles, you now see opportunity.

What had changed? Was it the characters, the events or circumstances in the example? No, the example and the "story" remained exactly the same. However you, the reader, are no longer the same person as the one who read the example months or years ago. It's as if you're a "new" person looking at the same picture, and are now seeing something different.

A similar thing happens with the books you read, too. The message which the writer wished to convey may not have been easily absorbed during the first reading. Its concept may have initially appeared too complex and difficult to grasp. It is as if our mind is dry and hard ground.

Secondly, the author is presenting his knowledge and experience - derived from investing a substantial amount of time and effort - for the benefit of his readers in a very concise form. The author may have spent many years researching, practicing, making mistakes and making course corrections. However since the author usually just presents his findings or "the way" without a detailed blow-by-blow account, what he says or suggests may sound absurd or implausible for someone just starting out. Whenever we feel this way, we need to remember the author had taken substantial time and effort to reach the position where he is able to practice what is said in the book.

That is why one must implement the change gradually and return to the same book to gain better understanding. On subsequent readings, the very same concepts may now become comprehensible and logical. And it is as if our mind is now fertile and ready to accept the message conveyed. I believe that this is because if we start on the path of change, the experience we gain along the way will give flavour to words in the book, we begin to see what was hidden behind the incomprehensible. And we realise that what the author expounds is indeed possible.

The Primary Building Blocks of Life

There are four essentials principles that I would like to share with you. These principles can be applied by anyone, regardless of their age, social, economic, religious, race or gender.

They are by **no** means the only principles that one needs to learn in order to navigate through life successfully. There are a myriad principles and skills that we will need to pick up and master along the way. But these four foundational principles will ensure a **consistent** rate of success in whatever you do in life. Success ceases to be a trial-and-error affair. Can we live our lives without ever mastering these four principles? Yes, we can. But in the same way that a person can survive eating only hamburger, by choosing not to master these principles would mean that the quality and experience of our life will be materially affected. In fact, if we learn to apply these principles early on, it will make the learning and application of other life skills more effective. Why? Because our application of the other life skills would be more goal-oriented and will yield quicker and more consistent results. It's like taking out a whole set of variables out of life's equation.

The four principles can be summarised as follows:-

1. **We can change our lives by changing our thoughts and the way we think**

    We are what we thing about. This is the principle enunciated by Napoleon Hill in his classic book *"Think and Grow Rich"*. We are at any moment the sum of all the thoughts that we have had in the past, up to that point in time. And we will (in the future) become the sum of all the thoughts that we have **now**.

2. **Our thoughts *can* become reality**

   Corollary to the first principle, just as we can manifest change in ourselves by changing the way we think, we can manifest our thoughts and ideas into physical reality as well. This is a very profound and exciting concept, as it means that firstly, we have the ability to create the environment that we live or work in, and secondly, we can also create the things that hitherto only resides in our imagination.

3. **Set clear written goals**

   To achieve anything, we must first determine what is our end state. And that's what a goal does: it sets a target that we aim at. Once we have set our destination, we chart the course, set the milestones and deadlines by which we will arrive at our goal.

4. **Take conscious, consistent & persistent action**

   Last but not least, we need to take action to manifest whatever we wish into existence. Without action, the other three principles will be for naught.

Although I have set out the four principles in this order so as to create a logical progression, this does not mean that any one is more important the another. All four are equally important and it is imperative to master them all.

These principles are not novel, and have been expounded since ancient times. If you read enough self-help, psychology, management, and self-improvement literature, you will notice that a common thread runs through all messages in these books: they consistently reiterate these four principles (whether individually or in a combination of two or more). The authors may present their ideas differently and cite different examples to illustrate their points, but the principles remain the same.

If our lives can be likened to a building, the four principles are like the three important individuals in the inception, design and construction of the building, namely the architect, the engineer and the workman.

Analogy of the architect, the engineer and the workman

The first and second principles are represented by the architect, who creates an image of how the building will look like when it's finished. The size, quality and grandeur of the building is limited only by the architect's imagination. In the same way, the better the quality of our attitude and beliefs, the grander and finer the 'structure' of our life will be. The third principle is represented by the engineer who, based on the vision, creates the framework of the building. He charts out the steps that are necessary to make the vision (an idea) into a physical reality. The workman represents fourth principle. He carries out the actual task of building, relying on the directions of the engineer, but always keeping an eye on the overall design presented by the architect. For the building to become a reality, all three parties must play a role, working hand-in-hand with one another.

In this analogy, the architect represents the visionary, establishing the primary concepts and ideas. Without the engineer and workman, the architect's ideas remain just a vision. An amorphous thought without physical presence. No matter how grand and ambitious his ideas may be, they are of no value whatsoever without the engineer and workman.

The engineer, working in isolation, can design plans for everything but without any no way to implement them, these plans will amount to nothing. It's like a book with an incoherent title, a table of contents, and without any actual content between the covers. We only see a bare framework and yet not truly know what it is supposed to be, since it was prepared without any thought of the end result (which only the architect provides).

Lastly - and we find this occurring very frequently in real life - is the situation where the workman works without any vision or plans. There is a lot of busy-work but very little practical results to show for all the effort. Although the workman may be able to produce results that are tangible, but without the benefit of a vision and plans, the results are haphazard and chaotic. His endeavours only leads to confusion, mistakes, frustration and disappointment. Over time the workman embarks on half-hearted attempts that are unlikely to be completed. Lives lived this way often cause people to wonder why, despite all their effort and best intentions, their life's work yield little result of note.

Just as applying one principle in isolation will not bring about success, a shortcoming in any of the principle will manifest itself in the quality of our life. For instance, if we are weak in the 'action' department, it's like having a grand building built on the foundation of great planning, but with bad workmanship. Therefore to be effective, all four principles have to be equally strong.

We are all made up differently. We aren't all strong or weak in the same areas. For instance, some of us may excel in goal-setting. We can write down in great detail why we want a certain goal, and how it would improve our life. We list down the steps and milestones to getting there. We can even detail out the resources we'd need. But then we never ever actually take any action. Conversely some of us may be great in taking action. We are game for any form of physical challenges and demands. However because we don't put any prior thought into the reasons, goals, and milestones, all that action yields little results.

We can also have a third situation where we have goal-setting and action principles down pat. Yet somehow we never ever get to the next level simply because we have limiting beliefs, and we subconsciously sabotage our efforts. To improve, we have to be aware of the areas that we are weak in. Only then can we focus on improving these areas.

The four principles are relevant in all aspects of life. However let's use an example would be close to many of our hearts - financial independence.

The four principles in action - Financial planning.

For many, attaining financial independence would feature as one of life's main goals. Financial planning is a daunting and complex task. It is one of life's project that requires substantial amounts of discipline, commitment and persistence to achieve. This is where a firm grasp of, and the proper application of the four principles is vital.

First and foremost one needs to have the correct attitude and beliefs regarding money, investing, and work. For instance, if you believe that money is the root of all evil, then you might become conflicted as to whether the pursuit of financial independence is something that is consistent with your personal values. Therefore you may need to change your beliefs regarding money and adopt new beliefs that are consistent with your goal to achieve financial independence.

Using the principle that your ideas can become things, you create a mental image of the standard and quality of life you associate with attaining financial independence, namely what your lifestyle would be, what you would do with your free time, where you'd go for your holidays, what are your hobbies, and perhaps how you will contribute back to your fellow human beings. Generate the positive emotions and experiential feedback that you will associate with this quality of life.

The proper attitude and state of mind is also necessary to enable you to persevere. Otherwise it's very likely that you will stray from your goal at the first signs of difficulty or temptation. What will make you hold true to you decision to consistently set aside money to invest whenever a sale comes along? If everyone has the very latest mobile phone or gadget, what will hold you back from getting one yourself?

Secondly, you will need to prepare a detailed plan laying out the milestones and sub-goals. Writing down your financial goals as clearly as you can will ensure that your heading in the right direction as you're going along. Without a clear and specific plan, you are constructing a house without blueprints. You have no assurance that your efforts will yield results.

Finally, having an empowering mindset and a well-crafted financial plan alone will not get you an inch closer to financial independence if you do not take any action. And once you have started, to commit to persistent and continuous action until the goal is achieved.

It's really easy to see how the process of having a positive mindset, setting goals and taking action can be applied, regardless of whether it is a simple task or a complex project. Once this process becomes second nature to you, you will begin to see a much higher rate of success and better quality results in everything that you undertake.

In the next chapter, I will talk about the first principle where we discover that who we are now and who we *want* to be have their genesis in the gray matter between our ears.

PART 1

We are the product of our thoughts

"We become what we think about"

This six word sentence encapsulates the essence of Napoleon Hill's classic "Think and Grow Rich". This is truly a profound statement in spite of its simplicity and brevity. It emphasises the power of our intangible thoughts, even we seldom attach any importance to the way we think and what we think about. For the purposes of this chapter, I will use the word "thought" broadly to mean our beliefs, attitude, and though process.

If this is the very first time that you've heard of this phrase, what it suggests may be contrary to what you have believed to be the truth, namely that we are the result of extrinsic forces and circumstances rather than our thoughts. However if you take the time to reflect on it, you will accept the truth of this simple statement.

You are, as of now, the sum of all the thoughts that you have had in the past, right up to this moment. Your thoughts fashions every facet of your life both intrinsically (such as your outlook in life, emotions, confidence) and extrinsically (your physiology, your body language, even the way you dress). Your mindset determines who you socialise with and the quality of your relationships with your loved ones, family members, and friends. Your thoughts have played a part in determining the type of house you live in, the clothes you wear and the car you drive. They even influence the work that you do, what you do in your spare time, even the television programs you watch.

The future will be a consequence of your past and present thoughts. This is an exciting revelation since it means our future does not lie in the domain of clairvoyants, and subject to the alignment of stars and superstition. Rather the future can be a well-lit and well-charted course to a destination of our choice. And it based simply on the choices we make what our choices and our actions right now. In the present. The future ceases to be the domain of fortune tellers peering into crystal ball, rather it is a consequence of our thoughts and actions in the present.

Change then boils down to two essential choices. Choosing how we interpret events or situations in our life and secondly, choosing how to respond or act.

It is our thoughts, not extrinsic circumstances beyond our control that truly determine what we can achieve in life.

Thoughts becoming visible

We can see the mindset, beliefs and thought processes of a person simply by observing what his present reality and life experience is. A person who habitually dwells in negative, limiting thinking experiences a life of perceived scarcity and limitations. He sees his dreams as difficult, if not impossible, to attain. Life seems full of dead ends and closed doors. As a result, he might feel disappointed and frustrated with life. His physical appearance and demeanour will also reflect his mindset. A person with a negative outlook will usually walk and behave as if the weight of the world is upon his shoulders. His speech and the words he uses likewise reflect his view of scarcity and limitations. Suggestions on how to improve his lot in life will be trivialized or rejected outright as being unrealistic or too difficult to achieve.

On the other hand, a person who looks at life in a positive light and abundance encounters a markedly different life experience. He will see opportunities abound at every corner. It is reflected in the confident air that he has about him, and in the light and lively way he carries himself. And the boundless passion, energy and enthusiasm for life shows in his voice. Even obstacles and difficulties will accord a positive-minded person opportunities to learn and to expand his abilities. He does not resent or feel jealous, but revels in the success of others and knows that he too, can achieve greatness in life. He understands that his life goals are already achieved, and just waiting for him to arrive at it.

> What you're doing today, right now, is defining your future. What you choose to do. How you choose to do it. When you choose to do it. All have an impact on your life. And it expands outwardly to the lives of the people around you.

Your beliefs determine what you think you're capable of

Your perceived abilities are determined by your personal beliefs of what the limits of your abilities are. This is a logical conclusion since, if we think that it's beyond our reach, then it's impossible. This is sometimes referred to as our "comfort zone". However occasionally we encounter a crisis that forces us to stretch ourselves beyond what we thought was humanly possible. After the crisis is over - and if we are aware of what had happened - we realise how much we had underestimated our true potential. Going a step further we might even realise how these self-imposed limits have affected our quality of life. Never take our beliefs, whatever they may be about, for granted. We don't have to wait for a crisis to happen to go beyond our comfort zone.

> The two primary choices
> - How we choose to interpret the events of our lives; and
> - How we choose to respond and act.

Taking control of our thoughts

Because of the deep and far-reaching effect that our thoughts have on our lives and the quality of our life experiences, the first crucial step in our journey of self-improvement is to take charge of **what** and **how** we think. This is the first foundation we need to lay down when building the life of our dreams.

If we are this moment, the sum of all thoughts that we have had right up to this moment, who do you want to be ten years from now? If you continue to have the very same type and quality of the thoughts that you have had all this while, then you are likely to remain the same person in ten years' time. Only that you will be ten years older. You can't become a better person without changing your mindset and the way you think.

If you aren't satisfied with the quality of life you've been experiencing thus far, you can alter the course and the quality of your life by changing the way we think. You *can* take yourself out of the situation you are in. You don't have to accept the situation. You *have* a choice. If you're thinking, "I have a choice about what goes on in my head?", the answer is "yes", you do. And the faster you understand and master this concept, the sooner the process of self-improvement gets underway.

What is truly exciting of the principle "we become what we think about is" that if we aren't happy with the life we have, we need only change our thoughts and the way we think. That change is within our control. We can make that change this very instant. And it's free! There are no clubs to join or fees to pay.

What you allow into your mind is as important as what you put into your body. There has been tons of research and literature on how the food we consume affects our health. We measure our caloric intake, the benefits of vitamins, supplements and so on. Yet we pay almost no heed to the quality of the information we allow into our minds by way of the books we read, the television programs we watch, the websites we surf on the Internet. Invariably the negative, unproductive content we consume will have undesired effects on our beliefs, attitudes and thought process. We will unconsciously adopt and apply that which we allow into our minds on a consistent basis.

People who succeed are careful of what they allow into their head. Since mental input can come from a variety of sources, they are mindful of what they read, what they talk about, who they mix interact with and how they spend their time. They are even mindful of the way they think, and how they interpret life events. So what you allow into your mind deserves your closest scrutiny and discretion. It's vital to reflect on whether the values, beliefs and attitudes we read in books, magazines, on the Internet, or listen to on the radio, podcasts, etc., are worth adopting.

Be conscious of how you perceive and interpret the world and life situations

In a nutshell, we consciously choose to (i) think in a positive way (ii) look at and perceive the circumstances in our lives in a positive way (iii) and consciously train our mind to shift from a negative mindset to a positive one. Every mental activity, however insignificant, leaves an impression. Individually they may seem inconsequential. However over time their collective influence is significant.

> "When there is no enemy within, the enemies outside cannot hurt you" - African proverb

This is a new way of life that needs constant vigilance and practice. Just like a little seed, your thoughts will grow and manifest outwardly in your physical appearance, your speech, your actions as well as your life experience. Just as a pebble thrown into a still pool of water will cause a ripple to go out to all parts of the pool, a change in your thought patterns will ripple out into all parts of your life as well, often in unexpected ways.

You may think that adopting a positive mindset is not a "realistic" way of going through life, seeing how difficult and hard life can be. But no matter how hard life may seem, you will agree that from time to time, good things have come your way. In fact, let's consider the converse situation. Is a purely pessimistic and limiting outlook "realistic" and will it make it easier for you to navigate through life? Hardly. I am merely inviting you to to be open to the idea that we do have a choice of how we look at life events. If having a pessimistic and limiting outlook has not been working out for you, then what do you have to lose by changing your mindset? You may come to realise that what is "realistic" is actually a mental construct. "Realistic" isn't about whether it is possible or not. It's whether you are prepared to do what's necessary to achieve it. If you are, everything will come within the realm of possibility.

> THOUGHTS => DECISIONS => ACTIONS =>
> CHARACTER => DESTINY

We are sculptors of our lives

It is said that when Michelangelo was asked how he had created David out of a slab of marble that other artisans had already worked on and abandoned, Michelangelo replied that David was already in the slab of marble. All he did was to remove the parts that weren't David.

Whether we are aware of it or not, we are sculptors of our lives. Do we, like Michelangelo, have a vision of what our life is about and go about working on it until our actual life mirrors our vision? Or because of a lack of personal conviction (or plain laziness) we allow our parents, peers, friends, colleagues or even the community we live in to dictate what, when, and how we do anything? Or perhaps, which I think happens frequently, we just take up the hammer and chisel and begin working on our life and see what eventually turns up as we go along. It isn't surprising then how lives fashioned in this way become quite different from who we truly are as individuals.

There could even be situations where we start off with a vision, but we settle for what life's circumstances permit. Just like a sculptor who starts off, intending to create a statuette, but during the process accidentally chips off some pieces and settles for a paperweight instead. A life created this way feels like it's compromised, because we have denied ourselves the chance to live life fully. Frustration and bitterness usually follow.

So don't be content to allow life to take you where it wants to go. Take control of your life, and make it go where **you** want to. You might ask "but what if life doesn't want to go where I want it to?". The thing is, this has never happened before. Life will **always** go where you want to. You just need to put in the effort and diligence. Don't be misled into thinking that it will require gigantic sacrifices and effort. You can start small, taking little steps. What is important is that you need to **continue** to take these steps. Consistency and resilience will trump most obstacles that we will encounter along the way. Take heart in the fact that many have walked this path before you, and they have made it. We would still be living in the dark if Thomas Edison had given up after considering the enormity of the task of testing thousands of different materials to find a suitable filament for the light bulb!

> **Remember:**
> - We are sculptors of our own lives. It is truly a great and precious gift which we ought not waste;
> - We <u>must</u> have a <u>vision</u> of what it is our lives are about. We must understand why that vision significant to us. This vision is unique to each of us, and the world is poorer place if we are just clones of each other;

- Always allow your vision to guide you. Use it as a signpost so you never deviate too far from your vision. Never give up, or stop working on your life. If you don't do it, no one else can, or will;
- Don't be content to just let life pass and see what comes along. You can control what you want your life to be, its meaning, and the quality of the experiences;
- We must never be content to compromise;
- Don't allow others to dictate who we become;
- Don't be too bothered about what others may think. Ultimately we are the ones who will live with the consequences of the life we sculpt. We can't trade it in, or get some else to live it. If it's something that you don't find yourself enjoying, then why do it?
- Negative thoughts, doubts and fears will always pop up. The more you push them way, the more they clamouring for your attention. We can to ignore them.

Now is your time to step up to the plate and take your place in the sun. Take charge of your life, and all the fantastic and wonderful adventures it has in store are just waiting to reveal themselves! So now that you're convinced that you can make that change, and you're prepared to give it a try. So how do you go about it? In the same what we develop the other parts of our body, we develop a new mindset and way of thinking through regular, consistent use.

Our brain is a "muscle"

Our brain can be likened to a muscle, albeit it can't do any work on its own. However unlike our physical muscles that have finite abilities, our mental capacity to reason, analyse and be creative are infinite. We can, by putting in diligent effort, improve these abilities. We are never too young or too old to start. Just as we develop our endurance, stamina and physical strength, our brain can be trained and developed too.

Initially when we first truly begin using our grey cells, we may feel its abilities are weak and we quickly become easily tired. And in the same way that you will experience tiredness, aches and pains when you begin a new exercise regime, you will experience the mental equivalent of such discomfort in your mental 'workout'. If you persist, you find yourself becoming more adept in analysing and thinking critically. And your mental "stamina" and "pain" threshold will be improve too. How far you can develop your mental abilities is the same as the extent to which you can develop your body's muscles. Whatever that holds you back from becoming physically fitter e.g. laziness, excuses, inertia will likewise keep you from developing your mental faculties.

Let's consider the role that our beliefs play in our lives.

Beliefs as a way of making sense of the world

> "Belief - noun- an acceptance that something exists or is true, especially one without proof"
> – Oxford English Dictionary

Neuroscientists conducting research on the human brain discovered that the brain works to make sense of the world based on our perception of what goes around us. In other words, the brain interprets what we perceive through our five senses (sight, hearing, touch, taste and smell) to come to a logical conclusion of what is happening. The mind creates a "story" to connect the dots. Hence the phrase "logical conclusion", which means a conclusion that the mind comes to. It's therefore possible to have a situation where two persons can experience the same life situation and come to two (or more) different "logical conclusions" of what that life situation was about, because each individual interpreted the same event differently. There is no one "right" or "wrong" conclusion. In the same way, beliefs are stories that we create to make sense of the world around us, the lives we lead and our identity.

Therefore if a belief is simply a creation of the mind, why don't we craft beliefs that are empowering rather disempowering? It is my view that in life, we can go through four possible stages of belief, although not everyone will experience all four stages.

Stage 1 Belief - The "Programming"

In Stage 1, we begin creating "stories" that help us rationalise the world around us. This takes place from a very young age. We perceive the world through our five senses and interpret the events according to a "If... then..." or a "Because... therefore..." explanations[1]. We also absorb wholesale the beliefs held by our parents, family and friends. These beliefs may also include accepted social, cultural and racial norms. We passively adopt these beliefs without thinking too much about them. Our mind is a blank canvas on which the people around us paint pictures of their fashioning. Without the benefit of any personal experience, we cannot refute the beliefs that others convey to us. Often we are unaware we even **have** a choice of rejecting these beliefs.

Hence we passively rely on the beliefs of others to explain the ways of the world. As we grow older, we begin fashioning beliefs of our own. We do so by relying on the information, experience and wisdom that we ourselves have gathered, and perhaps "layering" them on top of the beliefs that were passed down to us. Therefore in Stage 1, the world around us fashions the beliefs that we hold.

---

[1]   This is not to suggest that this is the *only* way that we make sense of the world.

Stage 2 Belief - The "Filtering"

In Stage 2, our beliefs become a security blanket on which we fall back on. Life events no longer form our beliefs. On the contrary, our beliefs now create our "reality". Our mind begins to "filter" or "interpret" life events so as to **reinforce** our beliefs. We choose (whether consciously or otherwise) to reject or place less emphasis on events or circumstances that are inconsistent with our beliefs. We will end up seeing only events that convince us that our interpretation of such events are correct.

After all, if we allow the beliefs that help us make sense of the world to be shaken, or destroyed altogether, what else would be certain in our world? How would we ever feel safe anymore? We therefore choose to see only what we want to see.

Through this filtering process, our beliefs become even stronger, as we "find" that life events do indeed support our beliefs. Our beliefs must therefore be correct! We seldom, if ever, question how these beliefs have come about, or how reasonable or rational the beliefs we hold so dearly are. Stages 1 and 2 are where most of us live the rest of our lives. However I would like to invite you to consider two other stages of our beliefs.

Stage 3 Belief - Bursting the Mental Construct

At this stage, we realise that all beliefs, whether we choose to label them good or bad, are simply mental constructs. They only exist in our minds. "Good" beliefs, empowering as they may be, are filtering out facts and events that are inconsistent with it thereby creating an imperfect reality. We can always find facts and circumstances that will be **consistent** with our beliefs. However in the same way, we can also find facts and circumstances that that disprove our positive beliefs!

Events of the world will take place as they must, regardless of the type and quality of beliefs that we have.

Our beliefs have no influence over these events; they only have an influence over how *we* perceive and respond to these events. By taking action based on the beliefs we hold, we will only yield results that fortify these beliefs. Our dependence on our beliefs is therefore an attachment to a mental construct that is unreal.

We must understand that there are (i) only events, (ii) our perception of these events without a need to label them as either good or bad, (iii) choosing to have an empowering attitude, and (v) making a conscious decision to take the necessary action to get us where we want to go. We cease to rely on a story told by our mind to "make sense" of the world. We are no longer prisoners of beliefs that others or we ourselves have fashioned. We also cease reacting to life situations automatically based on our beliefs, and instead act based on conscious, deliberate decisions that are premised on a positive attitude. By "positive attitude", I am referring to an attitude of possibility, a "can do" outlook where regardless of the challenges that lie before us, we will do whatever is necessary to make things work out.

"Good" vs "Bad" viewpoint

Let's say our car breaks down. We see a breakdown differently from a mechanic. We view the event as an annoyance that causes a disruption to our plans for the day. The mechanic on the other hand sees it as a job opportunity, a source of income. A good thing. Both we and the mechanic are viewing one and the same thing, and yet experience entirely different emotions from it. The emotions are therefore independent of the external circumstances, and dependent on how <u>we</u> perceive the event. Any event is therefore neutral by nature. An event manifests purely out a combination of circumstances, people and things. We <u>choose</u> to interpret the event in any way we want. We define the 'consequences' resulting from the event, and from there the emotions that come from the chosen 'consequences'. Good or bad, happy or otherwise.

Whereas our beliefs rely on past facts to substantiate itself, attitudes are a matter of conscious choice that we make **now**. Attitudes are not dependent on past events and experiences, and can be changed instantaneously. It is lighter ship to steer than compared to beliefs which, in order to change or come into existence, need (i) a "database" of new events or (ii) a re-look of past events and circumstances. A positive attitude is therefore a powerful tool to have when taking on new endeavours that we have no database previous experience to fall back on.

Stage 4 Belief - Emancipation from our beliefs

In Stage 4, beliefs no longer become a primary foundation of our life. Instead we elect to live based on a positive attitude towards our abilities and life as a whole. Of course, it is impossible to live life utterly devoid of any beliefs whatsoever. However our beliefs will only play a supporting role to our positive attitude. By being more conscious of the repository of beliefs we have, we can evaluate if these beliefs are indeed a true reflection of what is taking place in our lives. We can then consciously choose to accept or discard them. You might ask what beliefs should I have then? It is my view that you should adopt beliefs that will empower you and help you to achieve your life goals, whatever they may be.

Some points to reflect on:

- just because people have a different or even an opposing belief does not mean that they are wrong, stupid or ignorant;

- there are no "right" or "wrong" beliefs, since they are only mental constructs based on how we perceive the world;

- beliefs are never cast in stone and, as such, can be changed;

- between attitude and belief, choose to live from a position of attitude;
- if we choose to have beliefs, we should choose those that **empower** us to achieve our life goals.

Once you have filtered out and discarded the disempowering beliefs that you have held all our lives, two things are likely to happen. Firstly, you may realise and regret all the wasted times and opportunities because you were held back from achieving your full potential because of these disempowering beliefs. Secondly, you may also experience for the very first time a great sense of liberation. It's as if you have stepped out of the prison in you mind and are finally free to truly do what you aspire.

Attitude - change it and you change your life!

"Attitude" is defined by the Oxford Dictionary as "a settled way of thinking or feeling" or "a position of the body indicating a particular state of mind". In relation to the first principle, attitude is used to describe the former. It refers to a way of thinking and acting that independent of our beliefs.

We usually have very little regard to how great an influence our attitudes have on our lives. It is because of this ignorance, and our failure to harness its great powers that we don't experience consistent success. By adopting a positive and empowering attitude, we take charge of our lives. Our lives cease to be determined by extrinsic forces: how we were brought up, or our past or the people around us,.

This is a profound contradiction to what we may have previously been led to believe, namely that who we are is a direct result of genetical heritage or the socio-economic circumstances which we are born into. Having a positive attitude means telling ourselves that whilst we may not have had a say where our starting position in the race of life is, however we **do** have a say on (i) which race to join (ii) where the finish line is and most importantly, (iii) how we get to the finish line. The starting post has no bearing whatsoever over any of these three elements.

We all have heard at one time or another inspiring stories of individuals who have been born into difficult circumstances in life, and yet have gone on to become very wealthy and achieve great success. On the other hand, we will also know of people who have been born with a silver spoon in their mouth, and yet have achieved nothing of great importance. The individuals in the former situation adopted an attitude of possibility and a positive outlook in life in spite of receiving the short end of the stick. Their positive attitude created resilience, an ability to bounce back from failure faster. They did not allow their difficult life situations, be it abject poverty, a lack of formal education, or a physical handicap to stop them. And life rewarded them accordingly. Our genetics and socio-economic background are irrelevant to what we can be. Our future lies in our own hands. We can change its direction at will.

> "I learned this, at least, by my experiment: that if one advances confidently in the direction of his dreams, and endeavours to live the life which he has imagined, he will meet with a success unexpected in common hours." - Henry David Thoreau

Use empowering words

Adopting an empowering mindset includes remembering to phrase your thoughts in the positive, rather than the negative.

The trick is to not say "I shall not think of a negative thought". This will just cause your mind to focus on what you want to avoid! Instead, replace that thought with a positive one. The mind cannot focus on two opposing thoughts at the same time. Make use of this.

What's on your mind's playlist?

Choose:

- "I want [---]", rather than "I don't want [---]";
- "How can I achieve [----]" rather than "I'll never achieve [---]";
- "I can do this!" rather than 'I'll never be good enough',
- "If he can do it, so can I", instead of "Oh, he's so lucky" or "Oh well, success is for someone else...".

When you use adopt this new way of thinking, do it with certainty. With conviction. And with feeling. Feel the positive emotions in your whole being when you say them, and not just repeat it like a tired platitude. We are priming the mind and body for success. We will see later on in Part 3 how our emotions have a material bearing on our goals.

Be ever watchful of the mind's devious attempts to move back to negativity. Consciously move it away. If it helps, you can also "distract" the mind by focusing on other unrelated subject matters or activities that had brought up the negativity in the first place. Over time the mind is able to quickly become aware whenever a negative thought pops up. It will automatically know that it's not good for you, and be able to "flush" it out effortlessly.

"What the mind thinks about expands" – Dr. Wayne Dyer

It takes considerable practice for this new attitude to become an ingrained habit and that's what you're working towards. If practiced often and diligently, the positive thought processes will eventually become second nature. This is a mindset, that once mastered, will truly set you apart from others.

An Attitude of Assertiveness and Possibility

Assertiveness will play a crucial role in your initial stages of self-improvement. We encounter formidable foes: fear, self-doubt, bad habits, and a very small comfort zone. Last but not least, a mind with a mind of its own! If we can't tell ourselves to stay the course at times of adversity and hardship, no one else can. Others may lend a helping hand, but all the heavy lifting will need to be done by ourselves.

Assertiveness helps tame the wild horse that is our mind. Our mind will employ devious means to thwart our efforts. And it has a wide arsenal of means to do it. The mind will come up with a thousand and one reasons why it is too difficult, impossible or can't be done. But if we are assertive, in that we don't accept any of the excuses the mind comes up with and insist on the goal, the mind will eventually relent and start helping you get it. We must bring our mind into control and make it do our bidding, rather than the other way round. Once we have our mind under control, we will notice that fear and self-doubt slowly disappear. With a firm grip on our mind, it makes it easier to replace bad habits with habits that will empower us; allowing us to move towards our chosen life goals effectively and efficiently. We are also able to marshall the necessary resources to transcend and expand our comfort zone.

Assertiveness is not a do-it-once-and-forget-it event, but something we have to constantly remind ourselves to practise. Occasionally we may forget, but don't be discouraged. Just pick yourself up and try again. In time assertiveness will become second nature. Notice, acknowledge and celebrate small victories as you achieve them, as these add fuel to your confidence. Remember: our goal awaits us at the end of the journey. The better the tools that we have to help us along the way, the better our chances of reaching the end.

Be Assertive to Yourself

Talk and act as if you mean it. Walk as if you have a purpose. You have things to do and places to go. In whatever you do, do it as if what you produce makes a statement to yourself and the world of who you are, what are your values, and what you stand for. That attitude and physiology will be the framework that will support you to success.

You may have encountered individuals who, when they are talking to you, mumble as if they are talking to themselves and possess the posture of a person who's afraid of the world. Quite likely that person's mindset will match the physical appearance that we see: an individual who is unsure of himself and his place in the world. A man cowed by life's circumstances. On the other hand, we may have also met individuals who speak in an assured way, and possesses a strong, steady confident demeanour. They know what they're doing and where they're going. No matter what the obstacles, they are certain to overcome them. We are naturally drawn to such individuals, and have a greater sense of confidence in their ability to get things done.

The mind and body feed off each other. A confident mind causes the body to carry itself in a more assured demeanour. And acting confidently makes the mind more assured of itself. A win-win proposition.

Assertiveness does not mean being aggressive, mean, rude or unfriendly. It simply means an attitude of knowing what you want, and are undaunted in your efforts to get it. It also does not mean you have to be dishonest or unscrupulous in how you get to your goals. There are hundreds, if not thousands of ways in which we can achieve our goals legitimately. Why resort to the unsavoury ones? Assertiveness does not mean being brash, and possessing an outspoken arrogance. Assertiveness is equally at home in a state of quiet confidence. We need only know we can do it. Is there really a need to tell the rest of the world? Better, I say, to let our actions and conduct do the talking.

Beliefs

Re-evaluating our Beliefs

Let's consider some common beliefs that we may have which limit our ability to make the best of our lives. I would like to categorise them into three broad categories. These categories are by no means exhaustive. However it is a starting point from which you can do a personal assessment of your own sets of beliefs and determine if they actually help you towards attaining a better life. The categories are:

(i) our past and how it influences our present and future;
(ii) the beliefs imposed by others; and
(iii) our notions of success, and what it takes to succeed.

And as far as limiting self-beliefs are concerned, they can be broadly described as follows:

(i) they understate our true strengths and abilities;
(ii) they overestimate our limitations; and
(iii) they exaggerate the level of difficulty or the obstacles before us.

Our Past

How we allow our past to influence our present and future

We cannot underestimate the influence our beliefs formed during in past have on our lives. Very often these beliefs linger on long after the events that created them are gone. It is crucial that we understand our past merely plays a role that we *allow* it to. If we are ignorant of this fact, we end up unconsciously permitting our past to restrict the full potential of our present and future. To explain this, I will refer to two possible perspectives of what our past can be about.

It's important to distinguish between the events *per se* and the beliefs (mental construct) we attach to them. The events themselves are neutral in nature. However the beliefs we create from these events are the ones that we allow to influence our lives. For the purposes of our discussion in this section, we are focusing only on the beliefs.

First Perspective

In this first perspective, we believe that our past plays a very big influence in our lives. We use our past to justify and explain our current state of affairs. We may believe that our past, for instance our upbringing, our family, and social economic background has pretty much determined our course of life. It might even be events such as the death of a spouse, a marriage that didn't work out or a business that failed.

Things seem to be cast in stone. There is very little we can ever do to change our fate: a life of limitations and mediocrity. When we see others who are better off, we see it more as a consequence of being born at the right time and place, rather than effort and ability. Consequently we harbour a sense of resentment and jealousy against the people we deem "lucky". Since we believe that our fate in life is sealed, there's not much that can be improved on even if we tried. We stop trying. Not much can be done about the present, and the future looks worse.

Why we might hold on to a past that "limits" us

Sometimes we hold onto past events, especially the painful ones, like a badge of honour. We rely on them to remind ourselves and tell others of who we are. Our past **becomes** our identity. We are unwilling to let it go, perhaps out of fear that by letting it go, we will lose our identity. After all, if we aren't who we think we are, then who are we? And with the loss of this "identity", people may lose the sympathy they for us. Secondly, it may also feel as if one is stepping out into the unknown territory if the past is relinquished.

The past although a source of pain, is paradoxically also a comfort zone. A known evil. Thirdly, we could be relying on our past to justify for the sorry state that we are in now: an abusive childhood, a failed relationship, or a bad career choice. If the past is **not** holding us back, then what is? We are faced with the uncomfortable truth: that **we** are holding ourselves back.

By stubbornly holding on to our past as an excuse for the state and quality of our present lives, we lock ourselves out of the potentiality of a better future. We resist change so as to remain consistent to the story of our life, or the identity that we have created for ourselves. We are trapped in a prison of our own fashioning. It is only by letting go of our belief that the past has already determined our future, are we able to step out of this self-created prison. We choose to remain imprisoned or release ourselves. We hold the key.

Second Perspective

In the second perspective, our present and future have greater emphasis in our thoughts. When we discard our beliefs about how much influence our past actually has on our lives, we discard the notion that we are shackled to what had happened. We see that our past has no hold over us. What has happened has brought us to where we currently are **now** in life. It has no influence whatsoever as to where we will be in the future, unless we **allow** it to.

In this second perspective, options that were previously considered "impossible" or "off limits" are now on the table. Nothing is beyond our reach or abilities. And when we widen our options in the present, we can significantly alter the direction and quality of our future for the better.

We must accept that we can't change whatever that has happened. We can't "rewind" our life and change it for the better. Replaying events in the mind will not change anything. In order to get to where we want to be, we relinquish our attachment to past events, whether as an identity or an excuse. We will also have to discard the emotional baggage that goes along with it. We release all the hurts, disappointments, frustrations, anger and fears and let them return to where they belong: in the past.

Our past versus the unknown

Letting go, and not having our past to tell us what our "limits" are, is like entering into uncharted territory. It might feel like setting sail for the horizon, back when the earth was still believed to be flat.

This is a normal sensation. In fact, it is easiest at this point in time to run back to the comforts of our old way of thinking whenever we encounter the first signs of obstacles or difficulties. Because where we are now, unpleasant and self-defeating as it may be, is familiar and comfortable. As the saying goes, better the devil you know. Part of change is overcoming attachment to what is now. You have to act contrary to what the mind tells you is certain, and what is comfortable. Embrace the discomfort and uncertainty.

And maintain this new way of thinking, notwithstanding the obstacles that you will certainly meet. You have to initiate this process to go anywhere.

> The past cannot be changed, no matter how much we fret, regret, or worry about it. Even if we had all the power and money in the world, we will cannot change anything from our past.
>
> The future on the other hand is nebulous. The further out into the future, the greater the amount of uncertainty of what will take place. Once again, worry, money and power cannot guarantee with absolute certainty what will transpire.

The only one thing that is ever certain is the present moment. Within this present moment lies the magical ability to shape, fashion and direct our life in the direction that we want it to go. While we still cannot guarantee the eventual future outcome, however it does increase the likelihood of the desired outcome taking place. The more we place our hands on the steering wheel of life, the further we will head down the roads of our choosing.

Now is where we commit all our efforts and resources to realise our dreams. That is why the present moment is a truly precious gift as its name suggests. Don't dwell too often into the past (of what could have been) or the future (or what might be). Keep thoughts and attention firmly in the present moment, where they can make the greatest difference.

Beliefs imposed by others

Whether we care to admit it or not, we are conditioned by the beliefs that others have. They could have been passed on by our loved ones, family members, friends, colleagues and classmates. And where it concerns the things we do to succeed in life, they tend to share opinions, or we ourselves could adopt their opinions as benchmarks of what is possible. Very frequently their advice would be to avoid taking risks and taking the route that's tried and true. Is it therefore any surprise that very few of us ever take any real risks in life?

Don't allow another person's opinion of you become your reality

We see this happening when we see one person (and perhaps we are guilty of doing this ourselves) put another down by telling the latter is not smart, competent, smart, capable, etc. Don't allow another person's opinion determine what you are capable of doing, or becoming. That person's opinion or view will not become your reality unless **you** allow it to. We are **never** compelled by anyone or anything to think in a certain way. How we think and interpret events in our lives are entirely up to us. We get to choose our own reality. That is our innate God-given gift.

> "People who say it cannot be done should not interrupt those who are doing it."
> - George Bernard Shaw

Each individual's opinion on any matter is coloured by his personal circumstances and experience. Therefore no one can truly tell you what is the best that you can do, given your unique circumstances and experience except yourself. This is especially the case if that person has never attempted what you are planning to do! The other person's opinion, good as his intentions may be, could either be too ambitious or (more likely) too conservative. An outcome only becomes a reality if the mind chooses to accept it as a fact.

All children are born with an innate attitude of possibility. They are always willing to explore and try their hand at new things. Quite often it is the no's handed down by the parents and teachers that kill this natural enthusiasm and curiosity. For example, a child might be told that he has no ball sense and poor hand-eye coordination and, as a result, won't excel in sports. Due to his tender age, it's unlikely the child will be aware he has a choice of rejecting that opinion and accepts this statement wholesale. He forms a mental construct (a belief) of what the limits of his abilities are as far as sports is concerned.

If that child grows up into adulthood continuing to maintain that image, his "reality" of what his abilities are may forever be curtailed. The longer he holds that limiting belief, the stronger that belief will become as he will begin to find life situations that reinforce this belief.

If, on the other hand, the child is told at very young age that he has a choice to reject that limiting opinion, the child could have chosen **not** to believe that statement and persevere with his efforts. In time, he will overcome whatever initial shortcomings that he may have. He may not be able to perform at the level of a professional athlete, but he would have had a richer life if he had not denied himself the pleasure of taking up sports for recreational purposes.

We must constantly guard against beliefs about the limits of our personal abilities and weed them out. Always go on the premise that you **can** do it, and it **is** possible. And don't let anyone tell you otherwise! Whenever you attempt a new endeavour, don't tell yourself "I can't do that", "That looks difficult", or "I'm not going to do well in this". This is a negative reinforcement. Your mind is a very powerful tool. Whatever that you think, your mind will make it a reality. It never lets you down. If you say that you can't do something, your mind will ensure that you are not disappointed!

Don't measure yourself against another person's success

> "Always dream and shoot higher than you know you can do. Don't bother just to be better than your contemporaries or predecessors. Try to be better than yourself." - William Faulkner

Have you ever been in situations where your performance is compared with another's and found wanting? This could have happened when we were children and our parents were in the habit of comparing our academic achievements with other children's. We grow up feeling that we can never truly measure up to our parents' expectations. This belief - that we can never be good enough - can stay with us all through our lives. As a result, we are constantly comparing ourselves to others (and we would unconsciously find people who are "better" than us) and continue to find ourselves wanting.

Rather than use another person's performance as a yardstick, I would like to invite you to adopt an alternative viewpoint. Your only focus should be on the goal itself, and not what others have achieved. You only need to focus on your talents, abilities, and mindset.

Measuring how well you are doing by comparing yourself to others is like driving a car by looking only out of the side windows, and not through the front windshield. If we actually do this in real life, we are likely to be involved in a serious, possibly fatal, accident. We look out of the side windows for occasional references only, when it is necessary. Our main focus should be what is ahead, not what is happening beside you or behind you.

In the same way, measuring ourselves to others is not always a good gauge. Firstly, no two persons are mentally or physiologically identical. The person you are trying to measure up to may have strengths in areas that you do not. As a result, you may become discouraged as you are not progressing as fast as he or she is. However that is not the point. What is more important is that you should progress at a rate that is suitable to you. You should be interested only in your own personal progress, no matter how long it takes.

Secondly, the reverse may be true. The person whom you are comparing yourself to may be inferior in terms of his or her capabilities. Such a comparison may cause you <u>not</u> to perform to your absolute best abilities. This leads to complacency. Therefore other people's success should only be of passing interest. You alone are the one true benchmark.

True success is always a measure of oneself, for we may easily beat the yardsticks set by others. It's only when we question ourselves, in all sincerity, if we have done all that we could that we know if we had really given our all. Otherwise it will only be a pyrrhic victory.

<u>Don't let our own or other people's failure determine your chances of success</u>

To be honest, failure puts a dent in our confidence. With each instance of failure, whether in the same activity or others, causes us to subconsciously downgrade our assessment of our capabilities and chances of success.

We also do this unconscious assessment whenever we see others fail in the same activity that we have taken up or intend to take up. When we see others fail, we may believe that our chances of succeeding are likewise slim. Just as we shouldn't assess our chances of success based on our previous failures, we cannot allow other people's failures to determine our odds of success. If at all, we look at these failures only as a lesson, to determine where we or the others had gone wrong previously and determine how we can do it differently this time. We use the past failure as a stepping stone to success and not as a sign to stop trying.

Don't live other people's biases

Just as we don't adopt the limiting views others may have of us, we also must be careful about our beliefs about other people and the world around us. This includes rejecting the biases, prejudices and bigotry that our friends and family members have. Because in the same way you can find evidence to support these beliefs and prejudices, you can likewise find evidence to contradict these beliefs and prejudices.

Some beliefs and practices are brought out of superstition, ignorance or circumstances that may no longer hold true in the modern world. So it's important to ask why this belief is there and still being adopted. Is it still relevant? Is there a better alternative than blind unquestioning compliance? As always, the crucial question that we need to ask is: do these prejudices serve you and take you towards your life goals? If you have biases and prejudices do not serve you, remove them from your belief system.

Our notions what it needs to be successful

Failure is an outcome, not a description of who we are

This is a limiting belief that I think most of us have, and it is a belief we should discard as soon as possible. Our ego tends to associate the result of an event, be it a success or a failure, with who we are as a person. However we must be conscious that failure is merely an outcome to an event. It does not mean that you are a failure. You only become a failure if you choose to adopt that outcome as a state of being.

Failure hurts. It dents our confidence. And at times it is depressing to fail. But it's important not to beat ourselves up because of the failure. What is more important is what we take out of the "failure" and how we come out of that experience. Do we emerge from it defeated, weak and demoralised? Or do we come out of the event enlightened, optimistic and even more determined to succeed?

Forget the incident itself, but remember what the failure has taught you. Learn from each experience and strive to improve on what was done or omitted. What were the steps or procedures that could do with some improvements? If it's necessary to do a walkthrough so that the mistake isn't repeated in the future, do it. If it helps, write them out. I strongly advocate writing life's lessons down into a journal, as this brings matters into much sharper focus. It helps set out our accumulated knowledge and experience in a clear and accessible form.

Always remember that failure is an outcome. It does not become who you are. In fact the terms "failure" and "success" are mental constructs. What one person considers as a failure may be deemed a success by another! So what then really is "failure"?

54

Just as failure is an outcome, in the same way, success is an outcome too. It doesn't actually make you a "success" as a person. So we should never allow success to get to our heads, as we will become complacent and contented. See the success purely as a result of our efforts, and then direct our focus to new projects and goals.

Success is scarce

Another common belief is that success is only for a very select few. In order for one person to succeed, others must necessarily fail. Whilst this proposition may hold true in competitions where competitors are placed first, second and third, it does not apply to a vast majority of life's other activities and ventures.

The opportunity to succeed is abundant and unbounded. Another person's success does not deprive you of your chance at succeeding. For instance, the fact that your classmate is first in position does not mean that you are **less** intelligent or capable. Nor does it mean that you are **not** intelligent or capable. It does not mean that it is impossible for you to reach that pinnacle yourself. What it simply means is that he is first because he had worked hard, knew his stuff and was more consistent in answering correctly. And you too can be placed first if you yourself put in the effort, know your materials, and be more consistent.

Never for once think that another person is smarter or better qualified than you. You have all the same biological stuff that he or she is made of. It is simply a matter of directing your powerful mind towards your goal, for you to achieve it. It may not be a straightforward and easy journey. However it means that the paths are not closed off from you, thereby denying you the chance to achieve.

That others have gone before you and succeeded should be a source of inspiration and encouragement: that what you seek to do **is** possible. So you owe it to yourself to transform the way you think. You owe it to yourself to give it a try to be the best that you can be.

Let's all create a better world by taking ourselves out of a mindset of scarcity and limitation, and to believe that we indeed truly live in a world of abundance. We do not have to deny our fellow man his right to succeed so that we can succeed and flourish. How do we know this is so? Often times we open the newspaper and read that farmers in one country destroying their excess supply of vegetables or produce because the price these products fetched made them unjustifiable to be sold. Yet on the opposing page, you may come across an article of famine taking place in another country. The lack of any resources is not a result of scarcity, but of inefficient or improper distribution of resources.

Take a walk in any shopping mall. Look at all that there is to offer in the shops. The fact that the shops are without empty shelves means that there are more clothes, food, and household goods than people who want them! This implicitly tells us that the world is indeed abundant in its resources. It's just that we need to find a way to use and distribute these resources wisely and efficiently.

Let's be architects and builder of a better world for ourselves and our children.

Things will improve with a change of environment

Perhaps you've seen this happen before: people who leave the country, their jobs or relationships in the belief that with the change, they will have better prospects and a better life. They may believe that things will become better with the change of environment because the people in the new country, workplace or with whom they go into a relationship with would treat them better than how they are being treated now. The problems they face would magically disappear in the new environment.

However very often they will realise that the very same problems they used to encounter in the previous environment will start appearing in the new environment as well! This is because the "problems" they encounter are caused by internal factors, rather than external ones. These internal factors may be the mindsets, attitude, habits and beliefs that they have.

The people, whether in the new place or in the old one, are merely **reacting** to that his personality (his mindset, attitude, habits and beliefs). Therefore if his personality remains the same, people in the new environment will begin reacting in the same way as the people in the earlier environment.

In cases where a change of environment **did** improve the person's quality of life, it's usually because that person had also decided to undergo an internal change alongside the external one. But if he had been prepared to undergo the internal change in the first place, a change of environment would have been unnecessary. He could have experienced a better quality of life right where he was in the first place!

Therefore before you decide to "run away" from your problems, realise that your problems will just follow you. Face the problems you are encountering whether it's at home, in school, at work or in a relationship. Know what they are, and solve them. It may take no more than a change in the way you think. And very quickly you will notice a perceptible change in the way people react to you, and the surroundings as well. Situations may become more conducive and "flow" better, and you may even start getting "lucky breaks".

In that way you'd save the money from the trip, and end up with better human relationships, working conditions and a better life!

> People who succeed aren't people without problems. They have problems just like us. It's just that they have learnt to solve their problems. Consistently.

"It's not my fault"

As I said earlier, one reason we hold on to the past is because we use it to justify the state of our lives. We can explain to others that we are who we are, because of how we were brought up, or the circumstances in which we were raised. The past is just one of the excuses we rely on. When you're trying to describe the obstacles that are hindering you from achieving your goals, see how frequently it will refer to an external factor that is ostensibly out of your control. Ask yourself how this obstacle is holding you back. When you find the reason, ask yourself how **this** reason is holding you back. Continue this process with each explanation you can come up with. Often you will find that, at its core, the **true** obstacle is **internal** and it is well within our control. This is exercise of "peeling" away the layers of reason is a liberating exercise because we come to realise that there aren't any external factors that truly hold us back.

The truth is that you **are** responsible for **all** aspects of your life, the physical, mental, emotion and spiritual. Hoping that life will drop what you desire on your lap without any effort on your part is living life like a lottery. You are responsible even if you leave all decision-making in your life to others, or if you live life from day-to-day, letting life take you where it wants to. Abdication **is** a choice.

Living life without wanting to assume responsibility is like owning a house with a garden, and letting the garden grow wild. The garden then becomes a little jungle teeming with creepy crawlies. You won't have anyone to blame if a snake should craw into the house and bite you. Life bites you when you suffer a heart attack because you haven't taken care of yourself. Life bites you if you get passed over for promotion or get laid off when you don't put in the effort to work for the promotion or to upgrade yourself.

Granted there may be life situations that **are** truly beyond your control. Nonetheless this should not be a cause for you to throw up your hands in despair and say "See! I told you it's not my fault!". It can still be overcome by making small changes to how we perceive and interpret the situation. You get to choose whether the situation is an obstacle or an opportunity. So take responsibility! Go where **you** want to go, and not where life takes you.

"Commiseration" - Feeling miserable as a community

Whine. That's what people most do when they're unhappy with their lives, but their condition is not compelling enough for them to want to change. So they put the blame on God, the government, the economy, their parents, their upbringing, and everything else except themselves. Such like-minded people often come together to complain. They revel in sharing their complaints and dissatisfaction, at times seeming to compete with one another to see who has it worse!

They share their dreams of what could have been "if things were only different". Yet they desire the end result without wanting to assume the risks and investing time and effort to get it. So they make their promises and resolutions. They part ways, only to meet up again in the not too distant future to repeat the process.

If the current course and trajectory of your lifestyle is not bringing you any happiness or contentment, re-assess how you are living your life. Cancel your subscription to the whiners' club. Whining and complaining are what most people are content to do. The question is: are you content to accept what most people are getting out of life?

We naturally desire the very best if we don't have to work to get it. But it's an immutable rule - life gives you back exactly what you put into it. The colours, the wealth of experiences, the encounters along the way, friendships and adventures all need your full committed participation. They can't be attained vicariously.

> Look at the world from a new perspective. Chart out how to get to your life goals and destinations, and a set a time frame by which you should complete each stage of your plan. Record the progress. Refer to the written plan or list regularly to keep yourself on track. Learn along the way. Most of all, enjoy the experience!

I don't deserve success either(!)

Ironic as it may seem, just as we feel that we don't deserve the failures, obstacles and problems in our lives, we may feel that we don't deserve the good things that come our way either! For instance, when we are given an opportunity to enjoy the good things in life, we might feel that unless we "own" the things or personally bring about the circumstances that make the experience possible, these experiences "don't count". We are undeserving of these experiences since they were not due to our own merits. We may think that it's too good to be true and the good times won't last.

If we program ourselves to think that good experiences must come only from our own efforts, we overlook the fact that we are experiencing the event. Consequently we don't notice and appreciate the many good things that do happen every day. We can overcome this belief by being in the present and being aware of the experience <u>as it is taking place</u>, and without considering whether we are deserving. All life situations, good or bad, happen as they must. Regardless of our personal judgment of whether we "deserve" it or not. Most of all, be grateful for our blessings, in whatever form they may come.

"Successful" people are different

There are many popular notions of why "successful" people succeed. They are lucky, they are gifted or more talented than us, they were born into it, or they have the "right connections". The list goes on.

The fact is that "successful" people are not genetically different from the rest of us. They are physically identical to any other person on the street. Nor are they thrust into life with better fortunes, talents and opportunities. On the contrary, some of them may have started off in much harder conditions than ours. They encounter the same type of fears, worries, hardship and temptations, in one form or the other, in their life journey as well. Just like us. It's not as if they are blessed with less trials and tribulations, as a result of which they are able to achieve more than "ordinary" people.

The essential difference isn't the type or quality of life situations they encounter, but how they (1) perceive these events (2) how they anticipate or respond to these events, (3) what they learn out of these events, and (4) how much more committed they are to doing what is necessary to achieve their goals. You will notice that these attributes are psychological traits. In a nutshell, what separates the "successful" from the ordinary is the way they use the tool between the ears. Successful people <u>think</u> differently.

A very common example is the difference between how "successful" people and "normal" people react when they encounter failure. Often we would like to either forget the event altogether, or to use it solely as an excuse for self-pity and becoming depressed. However a successful person views failure as an opportunity to learn and to understand. They find out what had gone wrong in this instance and what could be done differently in future.

The successful person does not see the failure as a stain on his ego, or a testimony of who he is. He sees the failure simply as an outcome of the event. He resolves to overcome the issue, rather than to vow never to go near it again. They don't take it as a "no" or a "stop". They don't look at the failure as a sign from the divine that they aren't destined to achieve a particular goal. If they were to stop trying, it will be from a deliberate and conscious decision, rather than to rely on the failed attempt as an excuse.

Let's not misunderstand: everyone prefers success to failure. Failure hurts just as badly for a successful person just as for any other ordinary person. Successful people don't intentionally seek out failure. They don't set out expecting to fail. However if they do encounter failure, they treat the experience very differently.

Successful people maintain an upbeat mood and outlook no matter what the situation may be now. And needless to say, they will have mastered the four principles and many other aspects of their personal lives, whether they had done so consciously or otherwise.

There is no "successful" person who has had his success fall on his lap without hard work and adversity. Everyone puts in their dues to achieve success. Those who succeed are more likely to grind through the dreary and mundane routines to realise their goals, as compared to the ordinary person. The ordinary person would be more likely to give up half-way through the process or be distracted. These are the subtle but significant differences that we should emulate and to make them part of our mindset and lifestyle.

You can't be someone else by being who you are now

If you are not already progressing towards your goal, chances are you won't achieve them at the current course and trajectory of your life. You cannot become the person you want to be unless you adopt the mindset, beliefs, habits and lifestyle of your "ideal" person. In effect, you need to transform into a "new" person. Physically you would look and sound the same. But the mindset, beliefs, habits and lifestyle are that of another person altogether.

To be someone that you are aspiring to be, or to attain a desired life goal may mean having to live life in different way. It may also involve making decisions and changes that take you out of your comfort zone. If you can't do this, you may want to re-assess how badly you want to achieve your life goal, and if the goal is really something that you want. This would be cause to assess the reasons behind the goal you've set, and perhaps to find another reason that has a stronger experiential resonance. We will talk about experiential resonance in greater detail in the next chapter.

A common lament we hear is that life's unfair because it's dealt them difficult cards to play. Life is inherently fair, although the rules of the game may seen hard and unforgiving at times. But life gives back to you in the same measure as how much you commit into it. So take charge of life, and make the changes to truly become the person you want to be. You will realise that it's an exciting, meaningful and enriching experience being able to create events and experiences of your dreams.

> We can't experience any positive change from our status quo unless there's change. A change in our attitude. A change in the amount of time and resources we invest into our effort. In the way we think, what we do and how we do it. We can't be someone else by continuing to do what we've always been doing.

A successful life is built a day at a time

> "Drama is life with all the boring bits cut out."
> – Alfred Hitchcock

Alfred Hitchcock's statement reminds us that, unlike reel life, real life does not grant us a directorial discretion to remove all the mundane boring tedious parts to make it more bearable and exciting.

A successful life is rarely, if ever, achieved by a one-off event. There are no "overnight" successes. When we see a person enjoying the fruits of his success, we are merely seeing the tangible **results** of his efforts. We seldom see, or take notice of the time when that person is putting in the effort and working towards his goal. And because we don't see the substantial effort, resources and months, possibly years, that he has invested to achieve success, we assume that it was effortless and near instantaneous.

We often think that a successful life in terms of an event that happens when we have achieved something great. However a successful life is much more than one-off events. It is a process. One lives a successful life a day at a time. It is "built" in the same way a house is constructed; one brick at a time. So it begins with living a "successful" day: achieving what you set out to do for the day. Performing your daily tasks to the best of your abilities. Learning a new skill or acquiring new knowledge. Expanding your existing pool of abilities. Helping others, no matter how small or simple it may be. Being kind and courteous. Taking the time to be grateful for the day and its small blessings.

Just as the beach pebble is worn smooth by years and years of endless waves washing on it, our life goals are attained by carrying out the ostensibly mundane routines day after day. At times the changes are not visible. However it is through a long period of time that our efforts will eventually bear fruit. Just as the waves do not stop washing on the beach pebble, we must like persevere. Unlike a movie, real life cannot be rewound, paused or fast forwarded. We live it moment by moment. Good, fun parts as well as the difficult or monotonous ones.

Each day we are confronted with a series of decisions and choices in everything that we do. The choices we make take us either closer or further away from our goals. Therefore a "successful" day can be defined as a day where we make consistent, deliberate decisions and actions that achieve the former. We do this all our life and when we look back years from now, when we are enjoying the fruits of our labour, we will see that we had, indeed, led a successful life.

Remember, too, that one's life does not end upon achieving a major milestone. Never rest on your laurels. Once you have completed one life goal, relegate it to the past. Look forward to greater life goals, and things to do. Use your past achievements, knowledge and experience as springboards to propel you to greater heights.

Remember the feelings and emotions that you had when you completed a difficult and challenging task successfully. The happiness, satisfaction of completion, the rush or thrill. The peace of mind. And learn to use these same feelings and emotions when visualizing completion of the project at hand. Use your past memories and experiences in a positive and constructive way. Instead of perceptions of limitations, they serve you by improving your ability to accomplish goals consistently.

Patience smiles on those who wait

Being patient, good, honest and hard-working alone will not guarantee that you will achieve success. If you believe that these qualities alone are sufficient and, in time, you will be amply rewarded, think again. There are millions of patient, good, honest, hard-working people who wake up in the morning and work hard at their jobs, believing that in time, they too will be rewarded. They have been doing this for years, even decades, without ever attaining their goals. So this belief is flawed.

I am not suggesting that we should all abandon our good values and turn to a life of crime or live off ill-gotten gains! But I am inviting you to consider that in order for our honest efforts and hard work to truly bear fruit, we must direct our time, efforts and resources effectively. We will discuss more on time's role in success later on.

"It's never been done before" is not the same as "it's impossible"

These are two entirely different concepts although we often mistake them for being one and the same. Just because we've never tried skydiving doesn't mean that it's impossible. If we've never jet-skied, it doesn't mean that it's impossible.

If we look back throughout the course of history, man has always been limited by his self-imposed limitations. But it always takes a man or woman with a different perspective of things, to show that our cherished beliefs are not true.

Erik Weihenmayer became the first blind person to reach the summit of Mount Everest on 25th May 2001. He went on to complete the Seven Summits, namely climb and reach the summit of the highest mountains of each seven continents in September 2002. In March 2008, Anne Poole became the oldest woman in the United Kingdom to get a pilot's licence at the age of 65. Jim Warren of Vacaville, California earned his private pilot certificate at the age of 87 on 20th September 2010. At the time, he is believed to be the oldest person to qualify for a licence. On 20th January 2011, Laura Dekker set off from Dutch Carribean island of St Maarten to begin 27,000 nautical mile round-the-world trip aboard her sailboat name "Guppy". A year later she became the youngest person ever to sail alone around the globe.

"It's never been done before" is an invitation to us to transcend our comfort zone, and see what we are truly capable of. And when we do take up the challenge and succeed, we begin to question if "impossible" truly exists.

Conclusion

These are just some of the beliefs that we may have allowed to influence the way we live our lives. See the ways in which these beliefs may have held you back in certain aspects of your life or in life as whole. I hope that the beliefs I have listed above will prompt you to consider other limiting beliefs that you may have. With this awareness comes the ability to re-program our brains with empowering beliefs and attitude, the "software" needed for success. The mind is the foundry upon which all our life's success stories are born. Now that you have caught a glimpse of the true powers that your mind has, it's time to harness it and make your dreams come true. Start the process today. Start now.

PART 2

Manifesting what you visualise

"Thoughts become things." - Mike Dooley, *Notes from the Universe*[2]

As we have seen above, the qualities and attributes of what we desire, we can bring into existence by changing the way we think, including our attitude and beliefs. This in turn changes our behaviour and our actions. As a result of which, who we are and our life experience undergoes a change as well.

The wonderful thing is that we can also use the power of our thoughts to bring our ideas and vision into reality as well. This is not hocus-pocus. You *can* actualise thoughts. If you think about it (pun unintended), everything man-made once only existed in the mind of its creator or inventor. Everything that is around us today, this book, the clothes you are wearing, the furniture you are sitting on, and the very building that you are in now; from the tallest skyscraper to the smallest microchip ever built, only existed as a thought form at one point in time.

---

[2]   Author and speaker Mike Dooley has written a series of books that extensively cover the topic of how thoughts become reality. In particular, I would recommend his book entitled Infinite Possibilities: *The Art of Living Your Dreams*. It's a great read

And the best part is, each and every one of us has this ability. To illustrate, I would like to use the example of a cup of coffee again.

Whenever we want a cup of coffee, the desire first appears in our mind. The cup of coffee as at that moment has not come into existence yet. We take action either gathering the ingredients together and brewing the coffee ourselves, or we go to the nearest coffee shop to buy one. Either way, that cup of coffee was, until the thought came into your mind just disparate collection of ingredients: hot water, sugar, and coffee beans. In a very similar way, the "ingredients" (the materials, know-how, people and skills) for the physical or the intangible things that we desire are *already* in existence. We just have to take action to bring these "ingredients" together to turn our thoughts into reality.

The same process of actualising a cup of coffee can be used for bigger more complex idea, too. It may take more effort and resources to bring it into material form, but it can be done!

As at the time of writing, the world's tallest skyscraper is the Burj Khalifa in Dubai, United Arab Emirates. The Burj stands at 829.8 meters (2,722 feet). Its construction used 330,000 m3 (431,600 cu yd) of concrete and 39,000 tonnes of steel rebar, and it took 22 million man-hours to complete. The project involved more than 380 skilled engineers and on-site technicians.

Yet at one time, the Burj existed only as an idea in the mind of its design architect, Mr. Adrian D. Smith and a desire on the part of Emaar Properties to make the Burj a declaration of the emirate's capabilities.

Just as in the case of the cup of coffee, the "ingredients" for the construction of the Burj such as the raw materials (in the form of concrete, steel, lumber, cement, etc.) as well as the expertise (such as the architects, engineers, electricians, craftsmen and artisans) were already present. The developer had to bring all the raw materials and people together to make the skyscraper a reality. But it all always begins with a vision of the building in its fully completed state, and working towards it.

At the beginning of the project, the developer may only be able to estimate but not know exactly how many workers will be required, nor how much sand and cement would be needed. However by constantly making small adjustments and dealing with issues that arise along the way, the vision became a reality.

Therefore we can make use of the process of visualisation to manifest into reality both tangible things and intangibles (such as personal qualities, skills and abilities) in almost every aspect of our lives.

Methodology

So what are the common elements of turning the vision to reality?

- Having a goal in mind. Describe it with as much detail as possible. Understand why this goal resonates with you.
- Have a mental image of how the completed goal would look like, and the positive feelings that you will associate the end state.
- Have a written step-by-step plan on how to get there. A written plan ensures that you don't miss anything out. Secondly, it immediately makes your idea, which once only existed in your mind, take material form albeit in a list.
- Set deadlines by which each items in the plan are to be complete.
- List out the people whom you may need to approach to help with the project
- Ascertain if there any resources or materials necessary for the goal.
- Plan how the the various people and events are to come together.
- Working on the plan, checking off the items as they are completed and making changes along the way to accommodate contingencies.

The process that I have suggested suggestion above is not the only way to go about it. But I hope that it about it. However it does set out the main elements of a structured system.

Visualisation

The word "vision" when used to describe a goal is a very limiting word. It presupposes an end state which is perceived purely by sight alone. Hence the words "vision", "visualise" create a very one-dimensional "image". It's better to create an end-state that we can experience not just by how it looks, but how it sounds, feel, taste and even smell (the smell of success, anyone?). Beyond the five physical senses, the image of the end state should stir emotions within us. It may be a sense of completeness, accomplishment, satisfaction or peace of mind. When visualising, the image is that as if the goal has already been achieved, rather than something that is in the future. This is an important because the emotions and senses are mental constructs, the actual end-state need not actually have to be present in order for us to experience it. Somehow having a "vision" of the completed goal pulls us ever closer to it in real life. It helps us bridge the gap between what we deem impossible and the possible. The clearer and stronger that we can sense the end-state, the stronger the force compelling us towards it.

Having a truly engaging vision will also sustain us through the times of hardship that will inevitably come. While the logical reasons that justify our goals may fade and wither under the burden of pressure, hardship and difficulties, it will be the emotional, sensorial and experiential resonance that we we have with our goal is within us that which turn the tide of the battle in our favour.

Vision
The difference between those who succeed and those leading average lives is the quality and size of the vision they have of what their lives are about.

The power of visualisation

We all have had nightmares that felt so real. It might have been dreams of being chased, persecuted or attacked. The sensations were so real that we had to reassure ourselves that it was all just a dream when we woke up. Our hearts were racing, and the feeling of fear, urgency and anxiety was so real. Yet we were in the safe comforts of our bed throughout the whole experience.

What does this prove? That our minds create the pictures that we perceive, regardless of whether the picture is based on reality or not. And so what the mind can conceive in thought, it can similarly be manifested into physical form. The ideal job. The dream home. The fit, firm, taut body. The fantastic relationship. The <u>only</u> thing that prevents it from becoming a reality, is just another thought: that it can't be done. Remove that negative thought and let the mind do its magic!

This is why practising visualisation is important to the process of goal-setting. It harnesses the innate power of the mind to prime the body to achievement. Visualisation is not the same as day-dreaming as the former is a conscious and focused process that you direct.

When applying this process to achieving a goal or overcoming an obstacle, imagine yourself in the position **as if** you have already achieved the intended result. See yourself in your mind's eye as if you already successfully completed your task. If the task requires you to be in a certain place, imagine yourself in that place. And if the task involves other people, imagine their positive reaction to your successful completion of the task.

Imagine looking back at the times you had spent worrying and fretting, and laughing at yourself for creating such negative energies. We would have in the course of our lives come across a similar experience, where we have actually achieved the desired goal after some effort. Make use of this previous instance as an experiential reference point. Remember the emotions you had. The worries and fears that you may have had along the way.

Remember how it felt when you finally attained your goal. The sense of relief, happiness, and satisfaction. Remember also how it felt looking back at the worries and realising that most of those fears and worries never materialised. And those that did materialise were easily overcome. Apply these very same emotions to the present situation. Then act on the basis that the intended end result is already at the end of the journey. And that you need only to work on to reach it. A done deal!

Adopting this attitude gives us a sense of self-assuredness and confidence that our goal is attainable. And we need to just continue with persistence and commitment to arrive at it. This self-confidence gives us that little edge needed when we go about our lives and in how we deal with issues that crop up along the way.

Our confidence will show in our body language. We will talk and go about our affairs differently. And people will sense this, and treat us differently, as they are aware of your self-assuredness. The people dealing with us, especially our colleagues and subordinates are more inclined to be influenced as they are drawn by the strength of your conviction. This will make them more open to your suggestions and proposals.

And this effect will snowball, spurring you onward to feel and act ever more confidently. Self-doubt melts away, removing any unwarranted worries and fears that may otherwise hinder you. And most importantly, the mind would be focused on an image of success and of completion.

An Exercise in Making Thoughts Reality

For this exercise, make sure that you have at least few uninterrupted hours to carry it out from start to finish. It is important that the exercise must be taken to its full completion to be effective.

Take a picture of your bedroom or study or whichever room that you want to tidy up. Create a mental image of how you **want** the room to **be**. Visualise in your mind's eye how your belongings will be arranged, where the stationery will be kept, how you would want any ornaments, picture frames, and decorative items to be displayed. Now take a picture of the room as it is.

Start tidying the room. Begin packing things, perhaps in categories that they belong. Put the books together, stationery in their own stack. Whilst you're at it, take this opportunity to clean up the place as well. Wipe down any dusty areas. Pack things that you don't use frequently. Throw away any junk or unwanted items. Begin arranging and putting the things according to how your mental image was. Don't change your mental image as you go along. Just maintain it. The idea is to not vary your goals to make the process faster to complete, or the path easier to travel. Once you have finished, take a picture of the room.

Compare the "before" and "after" pictures. Note how the end results resemble the mental image that you had. This is just a simple exercise to prove that an intangible non-physical thought form that once only existed in your mind can manifest itself into reality.

Now also take this time to experience the feeling of completion. Feel the sense of satisfaction and achievement as you stand in the middle of the room and look around you. Recall also the feelings that you had whilst tidying the room. These emotions will be the reference points for future visualisation projects you take on. This exercise can be used with virtually any tasks that you may have. Practice with simple short physical tasks first, as what you are trying to do is to lay down a firm foundation of the process of visualisation and the steps to completing the task. Once you've become better at it, you can take on more complex and longer duration tasks. This will then challenge you to maintain the mental image over a longer period of time, and to hold firm to this image notwithstanding any obstacles or delays that may come up along the way.

Conclusion

If you've never had a vision of yourself beyond who you are right now, in other words, how you'd like your personality, work, relationships, lifestyle, and contributions to fellow human beings to be, perhaps it is time to dream a little. And if you have always known that you're meant to be more than you are now, to achieve greatness, then take this as an affirmation of your conviction, and that you can indeed make what's hitherto hidden a reality! And what a great and glorious adventure it will be for you!

In the next chapter, we will be looking into the second essential principle, that of goal-setting. Now that you see how a change in our beliefs system, attitude and thinking process opens up opportunities, let's see how we can chart the course towards the goals that are meaningful to us.

PART 3

Goals

Finding the Reason

We begin with this all important question: why?

Why do we want the goal that we are setting? The reason may be immediately obvious, and we are simply finding ways to bring the reason into reality. Yet at other times, the reason may not be so clear. You might even feel that there is more than one reason. It may also be entirely possible that we set goals solely for the sake of setting them without delving too deeply into the reasons behind them.

While the act of setting the goal is easy enough, however sticking to what needs to be done to attain them is another story altogether! To take the oft-used example: weight loss. Let's say you have a specific amount of weight that you want to lose, for instance 10 kilograms. However before you embark on this goal of weight loss, you must ask yourself do you even want to lose weight? Is it for aesthetic purposes? For health reasons? A better quality of life? Because it's fashionable? Or because you were told to do so?

Put another way, the goal is from the brain. The reason emanates from the heart. It is my view that our goal must (1) be tagged to a reason, and (2) the reason ought to be more than just a superficial one. In other words, tag it to a reason that resonates with you and which you want to satisfy **very** badly. Setting a goal can be likened to constructing a building. The bigger the goal, the taller the building.

And the taller the building, the deeper you will need to dig to establish a solid foundation. In the same way, we dig deeper into ourselves in order to attain higher goals. For we need to find the true reason that will anchor us when we encounter challenges, just as the building encounters strong winds and bad weather.

If you do not ask why and find a truly compelling reason before embarking on the goal, then when the goal demands sacrifices, causes you to go out of your comfort zone, or necessitates a commitment of resources and time that will force us to make painful choices, it will prompt us to inevitably ask "Why am I even doing this?", "Is this worth it?". Going back to our weight loss example, this happens whenever we encounter pain and discomfort during exercise, when it's raining and we don't feel like getting out of bed to get to the gym, when we are tired from a hard day's work and we just don't feel we have the energy. When we have to put off eating our favourite food in order to stay on our diet program. If you don't have a compelling reason to remind you why you need to stick to the exercise regime, in spite of so many other valid reasons not to do so, this will be when we start on the downward spiral of compromise. Eventually all efforts to keep to the regime will come to a halt. And we fail.

Having an overarching reason that resonates with you also helps make the decision-making process along the journey easier. Often we may be faced with options that are inherently suitable, and are hard put to come to a definite decision. In these situations, it helps to recall what our main reason is, and that may just help tilt the decision in favour of one choice over another.

There may be a myriad reasons that underlie our decisions to pursue any given goal. And there is likely to be many facets within each reason itself. If we peel off all the extraneous reasons like the layers of an onion, we will arrive at the core reason. Once we know the core reason, we can craft a goal that will **specifically** address this reason. We assured that once we achieve that goal, our needs are fulfilled.

In order discern this core reason, we can have to determine source of the reason (namely, where the reason emanates from), and the degree of importance that we attach to the reason. This can be looked at in the context of two sets of spectrums that I call (i) the Internal v External spectrum and (ii) a Aesthetic/Superficial v Fundamental spectrum. Understanding how these two spectrums will help us find the reason that has experiential resonance with us.

Internal v External reasons

Firstly, the source of the reasons behind our goals can be grouped into two categories, namely internal sources and external sources. By "internal" I am referring to reasons that emanate from within ourselves, and are largely within our control. A reason based on an "external" source is usually imposed on us by other people or external circumstances. Examples of such sources are fame and recognition, peer pressure, instructions from our superiors, our parents' wishes, or even a desire to achieve a goal to please someone we love.

It is my view that between the two, it is more effective to anchor our goals to reasons that emanate from within ourselves. External reasons are subject to many significant downsides. Firstly the question of whether we have successfully achieved our goals are determined by others. Secondly, the very definition of "success" itself is may be subject to differing meanings and interpretation, depending on who you ask. And very often we fail to even ask. For instance, if we set a goal to do something in order to be accepted by our peers, how would we know if the goal is "acceptable" by the group at large? Thirdly, reasons based on external factors are subject to fluctuation or change. Using the earlier example, what happens if the goal that we are working towards is no longer considered popular or fashionable? In short, externally based reasons is susceptible to uncertainty, doubt, and confusion. The more uncertain and unclear that a reason is, the greater the likelihood that we will not stay the course to achieving the goal. The less control we have over the reasons, the weaker their influence over us. Obviously pursuing - and never achieving - a stream of goals premised on ever changing reasons will adversely affect our confidence in taking on new ventures.

On the other hand, reasons that emanate from within ourselves are within **our** control. We define what constitutes success, and these parameters of success do not change, unless we choose to change them. We take **ownership** of the reasons. Consequently our reasons are clear and unequivocal. We are more committed to, and confident of achieving our goal. Therefore it is my view that we are more likely to achieve goals that are anchored to reasons that we create ourselves, rather than those imposed on us by external sources.

Superficial v Fundamental Reasons- Finding our experiential resonance

The "why" comes down to our senses, emotions and experience.

The other spectrum that we should consider how deep does the reason strike a chord with us. This ranges from the superficial or purely cosmetic (for instance, "I am dieting so as to look good") to the fundamental ("I want to diet so as to enjoy a better quality of life"). What may be a fundamental reason for one person may be a superficial one to another, because we each attach a different value to the same experience. Therefore another person may find that looking good is a fundamental reason whereas a better quality of life would fall into the superficial side of the spectrum. Again, there are no "right" or "wrong" answers to this.

A superficial answer to the question "why" begets superficial, half-hearted efforts; and this usually results in failure. Or at best, our efforts will not go beyond our comfort zone. The more convinced you are that your goal will improve your life experience, the more effort and commitment you will invest into the venture.

The experiential resonance

Upon deep reflection, we will realise that all fundamental reasons must engage us in the context of our life experience as human beings. Superficial reasons, on the other hand, do not engage us in that way. Hence in order to create a truly strong and persuasive reason, we need to find fundamental reason that will strike a chord with us experientially, or what I refer to as "experiential resonance".

By "experiential resonance", I am referring to that which engages us through all our 5 senses, our emotions (happiness, confidence, excitement, the sense of accomplishment, satisfaction, etc.), intellectually, spiritually and experientially (which is a composite of all the earlier elements)[3]. The greater the values we attach to the sensorial experience, emotionally as well as intellectually, the greater the resonance will be. Defined in this way, a positive resonance is one where you feel it in your whole being that that's the "right thing" to do. The resonance is so strong it may come over you as if it were an emotion in itself, as if you are at one with the Universe.

Some self-help books suggest attaching emotions to the goal. My submission is that, rather than just playing a supporting role, our emotions or experiential resonance is the very **basis** of the reason behind the goal.

Reasons with a strong positive experiential resonance will be both the immovable object that keeps us steadfast and the unstoppable force that keeps us moving in spite of the obstacles we face.

> In the context of goal-setting, "experience" refers to our own unique **interpretation** of the sensorial feedback we get from our senses whilst on route to our goal, or upon attaining the goal itself.

---

[3]   Throughout the rest of this book I will be frequently using the phrase "experiential resonance" to mean all the above mentioned elements.

> For instance, how do we describe the "experience" of a good restaurant? It's in the ambience, its decor and the lighting. It's in the cool crisp feel of the air itself. It's in the way the waiters attend to us and go about their tasks in a quiet unobtrusive manner. It's in the way the menu is presented. It's in the quality of the cutlery used. It's in the texture of the linen tablecloth. It's in the way the food smells, and tastes in our mouth. Finally it's in the satisfied feel we have after a really good meal.

The reasons must stir feelings that we can almost touch, hear or taste in our mouth. We need a reason to the "why" that's so intense and deeply ingrained emotionally that we will be able to say, "Oh yes, that's why..." and persevere. Or it might be that the reason is so strong that the "why am I even doing this" question **won't** even surface!

The reason serves both an anchor and magnet that will help you persevere through the hard bits of the journey. It will also determine the quality and magnitude of the effort in which you will put int towards attaining the goal. In other words, it will decide how high you will set the bar above average. The experiential resonance to adopting an exercise regime for (a) a person who merely reads that losing weight reduces the risk of a heart attack, and (b) a person whose doctor tells him that unless he loses weight, he may suffer a heart attack, and (c) a person who **actually** suffers a heart attack because of his weight problem all differ vastly. Hence their attitudes, inclination and intensity of their commitment towards losing weight will differ accordingly. Needless to say, the victim of a near death situation will see the most value for losing the excess weight.

The "why" question also has another benefit, namely it prompts you to ask if the goal you are setting will *actually* get you what you truly desire. In the weight-loss example, instead of setting a goal pertaining to exercise, it may involve a goal relating to diet and choice of food intake. It may even be a goal or goals involving both components. Therefore rather than blindly setting goals, by first asking "why" forces our minds to consider the available options, as well as to explore options that we may not have even considered. In fact, if we reflect and give this subject sufficient thought, we will realise that all reasons will eventually dovetail to how we want to live our lives, what we expect out of it, the experiences we want to have during this lifetime. So if we are able to answer these questions, the paths we choose to take, and the goals we set become clearer.

Finding a reason with a strong experiential resonance is crucial both in **initiating** action towards a life goal, as well as **maintaining** our efforts once we've started on the journey. The latter is important as, over time, the original reason may cease to have as strong a resonance as it did in the beginning. Consequently our commitment towards the effort will start to flag and fail. We may need to find a new reason that resonates with us now if we wish to persist with that goal.

Whatever we seek to do in life, is to bring our life experience into alignment with what we think our life is about at that given time. Why do I say "at that given time"? It's because the meaning we attach to life will likely change through the course of life. We may value one life aspect more than another at different times of our life. Therefore we will be constantly seeking to understand what resonates with us, and constantly setting goals that are consistent with our life purpose.

Therefore whenever we find that we are having problems maintaining our enthusiasm, examine if the reason behind the goal still resonates with you. If you not, you will need to find another reason that resonates with you to keep the momentum going.

A well-written goal tells you *what* you're going after. Knowing *why* you want to achieve that goal *keeps* you going in spite of what you will face.

'Why' - Take the time to answer

The question "why" should always be asked at a time of reflection, with an undistracted mind. It's best not to search for the underlying reasons whilst you are busy. Yes, brief glimpses and ideas could pop up in your mind, but what you should do is to jot them down quickly and flesh out these ideas later on during your quiet time.

Very often we make important decisions rashly, at inopportune moments. We chart courses for important life destinations without giving them the due consideration they deserve. For instance, how many of us truly take time to consider our choice(s) of career path? Or do we just accept whatever that comes along, as we need to earn a living? Or to make our parents proud? Or because all our friends are working in the same kind of jobs?

It is my view that when we make hasty decisions, we may end up with a job that we can't really commit to. We can't put all our heart and soul into it. This lack of commitment shows in the quality of our work. We live an unfulfilled life. We might finally decide that this is not the job we want after all, and quit. But if we continue to just pick and choose our jobs without thinking carefully, we end up repeating the whole process again. We waste precious time and resources. Little by little each wrong choice saps our enthusiasm towards our career and life as a whole. More importantly, our wrong choices dim our view of life. We look back and realise much of our life has passed us by, and we have nothing much to show for it. We feel doomed to a life without aim or purpose.

So is it all just about me?!

At this juncture, you might be thinking so it's all just about my own happiness, my own personal goals and my personal feelings? Isn't that self-centered? How does this make the world better? Isn't the world what it is today because of selfishness?

How do you reconcile personal happiness, self-actualisation with improving the world and the welfare of others?

I want to clarify two points. Firstly, the experiential resonance is purely a reference point by which we establish the reasons behind the goals we set. It's the signpost and anchor that helps us stay the course in our journey to success.

Secondly, this is not an exhortation to undertake only self-indulgent pursuits. Or that we will only find happiness and meaning in life by being purely "self"-ish. You will quickly realise that most self-indulgent pursuits don't really resonate with us at an emotional and experiential level. On the contrary, many of us will find a deep sense of emotional and experiential resonance when we're out and about helping and serving others! We don't live life alone. What we need out of life, and for living, we get it from others getting what they want. In creating our life's puzzle pieces and putting them into place, we will (i) come into contact with and (ii) need the help of and (iii) collaborate with other human beings who are also in *their* journey putting their life puzzle pieces together.

Looked at it in another perspective, we are helping each other to collectively climb up to a higher level of existence. We can only reach higher if the rest of our fellow human beings can come higher up with us, too. I can only become better if *you* become better too. How we can help others depend on what we can bring to the table. Within each of us is a reservoir of skills. Make use of these skills to serve and give value to others. It is my view that the more help we accord to others, we will acquire more of the means of reaching our goal. This is by no means mandatory, but let's see if the volume and quantity of our service to others does not result in a higher quality of life experience for ourselves!

Now that we understand the influence the reasons behind our goals have, let's consider the importance why setting goals, as a principle is vital to success.

Importance of goal-setting

It is one of the cornerstone to attaining the things we want in life It is one of the numbers to the combination lock to a great life. If you master and consistently use the principle of goal-setting, it is an edge that you will have over a large majority of our fellow human beings. Because even after being told or reading about it, few will truly attempt to lead a goal-driven life, as it takes too much effort, resources and sacrifice.

> Set down **your** plans to reach **your** goals. Because its **your** life, and **only** you know what will make you happy and accomplished.

Why it's important to set goals:

1. It acts as a compass to give you direction in life, and the mind has a clear picture of where to go. You can never "arrive" if you don't know where you're going;
2. You can prioritise the various and often competing demands on your time and resources;
3. Setting goals ensures a more **consistent** rate of success as your actions are no longer based on chance. It ceases to be a case of "try and hope for the best" and becomes "set the goal, get what you want";
4. You cease letting life take you where it wants to, but you take charge and decide where you want to go. In other words, life's experiences are determined solely by you, not by others or by life's circumstances. You are responsible for your own life, even if you choose to abdicate your right to choose. Therefore why waste that right?
5. It adds flavour to life. Life ceases to be a grey, dull existence that is full of drudgery and routine. Goals colour these routines and events, giving them a greater reason and

purpose. We travel along the road of our choice, knowing that good things await us at the end of our toil;

6. Goals stretch us. Often we work within the realm of our comfort zone, whatever size it may be. Setting ever more ambitious goals make us go beyond the boundaries of what we think are our physical and mental limits. At times the "expansion" comes in sudden noticeable ways, and at other times they come quietly and gradually. In either case, goals expand our capabilities.

The methodology of goal-setting

1. Define the goal and write it down. A clear and detailed goal eliminates ambiguity. It also allows you a method of assessing if you're making headway. As this is an important step, you must take the effort to do this. The time taken at this phase saves time correcting mis-steps later on.

2. Understand **why** achieving this particular goal is important to you. The reason must be intrinsic and has a strong experiential resonance. This is a reason that only you yourself can find. Know what it is you *really* want from the goal. It could be a "byproduct" and not the real source of motivation. If so, could this be achieved through other means?

3. Occasionally we may have more than one reason for the goal we set. In these situations, we may need to focus on one predominant reason, or at least understand that we possess differing reasons with potentially differing end-states for ostensibly the same goal. For instance, let's say you want to improve your game of golf. Do you want to play because it's your passion or be good enough to represent the club? Or to attain fame and fortune? Or are you doing it fulfil some other person's dream? While all these reasons are perfectly valid, focusing on one reason over the others helps to avert

any internal confusion as to whether (1) we are making progress (2) we are heading in the right direction and (3) we have reached our goal.

4. Once you've identified the reason that resonates with you, make sure that the goal you're setting will satisfy that reason. Will this goal actually take you to your desired fulfilment? Don't assume that once you have the reason, the goal will satisfy it, as another goal may be a better option. Otherwise you may experience frustration if you commit the time and effort to reach the goal but don't feel the sense of fulfilment and achievement. For instance, some people equate money to having more free time. But money may not necessarily bring about more fee time, as trying to earn more may engender spending more time at work.

   Try to understand why you want the additional time for. What are the activities that you want to take up? Might it be possible to take it up with your existing financial position?

5. Know what are the components necessary to achieving that goal - subgoals, the people involved, the necessary knowledge, skill sets, and experience. What you will need to change, or adopt to get there? For instance, changes to your attitude, belief and lifestyle;

6. A deadline is crucial so that you can measure progress. Otherwise the mind will be seduced into thinking that progress is being made, when it isn't. Set a time frame. One that is realistic, not too` short, but will nevertheless stretch you;

7. Keep a journal. Create a checklist if possible. Write down the lessons you learnt along the way. Write down your experiences. Take note of the obstacles you encountered and how they were overcome, or remain outstanding. Where possible, have a walkthrough of the processes. Take note of any new goals that the existing goal may create along the way;

8. Review your short-term and long-term goals from time to time to see if you are making progress. This is especially important for long-term goals was they are easily forgotten or set aside when you're mired in the details or day-to-day grind;

9. Re-look your goals over time. Are you getting nearer to it? Does it still have the same intrinsic connection or resonance as when you first started out? If not, re-assess the reason and goals again. This is why writing down your goals help. Change happens. So we have to change as well in order to lead meaningful lives;

10. The completion of each sub-goal is in itself an achievement. Feel the happiness and emotions of completing each sub-goal. Amplify the positive experience;

11. Constantly evaluate your approach. Ask yourself if this situation necessitates persistence or if it is necessary to effect a change. Find new ways to maintain your motivation and willpower. Strive to find ways to become more efficient and effective in the way you do things;

12. Visualise - this cannot be underrated. Replay the end-state in your mind from time to time. What you'd be saying. How you might feel, for instance confidence, a sense of fulfilment or even vindication. Remember to engage as many of your senses as possible in the exercise. The idea is to periodically re-connect with the experiential resonance that you have with the goal.

Defining "Success"

I define "success" as a temporal situation where we attain the target (or goal) we set. It is not a description of who we we are as a person, but a description of a situation where the elements necessary for reaching a goal have all come together.

Defined in this way, there are several significant implications:

- There must always be a goal. Without a target, we can't even begin!
- We must know what are the elements necessary to reach that goal.

ELEMENTS --> GOAL --> SUCCESS

- Defined as such, "success" will mean different things to different people because every person may have a different vision of what the end-state will like in any venture. Like beauty, success is in the eye of the beholder. It is therefore not possible to have an all-encompassing benchmark for success.
- To understand a person's definition of "success", we must first understand that person's definition of success.
- Success can even mean different things to the same person at different times.
- As success is merely a description of a situation that is transitory in nature, once achieved, it belongs to the past. Success may cease to be so if (1) the criterions are no longer met, or (2) when the criterions are changed - whether by our own volition or circumstances beyond our control.
- What we consider 'success' may by imposed by laid down by others, adopted, or laid down by us.
- On this basis, what some may consider as successful, may not be so, because different individuals take into consideration different factors when deciding whether success has been attained.
- To attain 'success' as a person, we may look to role models who have, in our opinion, reached the goal that we have similarly set.
- For a group setting out on a common goal, "success" must be defined and agreed upon beforehand. Otherwise each group

member will have a different interpretation of what "success" means. This can only lead to confusion, misunderstanding and conflict.

Developing the right mindset to goal-setting

- Don't be shy about either the process of setting goals or the goal itself. Don't feel embarrasses that it may sound foolish to others, as long as it's important to *you*;
- Don't let any excuse detract you from starting;
- It's never too early to start. Nor is it ever too late to start. Any notions of "too early" or "too late" are purely mental constructs;
- Don't wait to have "more experience" before doing it. The later in life that you start the process of goal-setting, the less experience you will have. In short, if you don't do it you won't have any!
- Take the time to think, reflect and decide. You must do this. There are no shortcuts here;
- Don't be afraid to get it wrong. It's alright to make mistakes. Take it as practice. We only become better when we make (and learn from) mistakes;
- Write your goals down. Describe it clearly and flesh it out with as much detail as you can. Describe how it would look and feel, if possible. Write down how this goal is significant to your life in a positive and empowering way. How does it change your life for the better? Elaborate on the emotions and experience it will bring to you.
- Elaborate on the reason for this goal. What are you getting out of it? Again don't be afraid to write down "simple" or "frivolous" reasons. But don't just stop there. Our very best ideas usually come when we persist at it. Discover what the primary reason is, that resonates with us at an experiential level. This step is crucial as it may reveal that your goal may not ultimately satisfy your primary reason;

- With sufficient practice, the reasons will become apparent first. Thereafter the goals themselves fall into place. Better planning skills come with practice, not with time or age. The more you do, the better you become;
- Goal-setting is a personal effort. You can share it and you may solicit other people's opinion. But you have to make that goal your own. The greater the intrinsic connection, the stronger the motivation you'd have to achieve it. It's for this reason that you should not adopt the goals of others as your own. Remember that a lot of people, especially parents, want to "imprint" what they have not achieved or missed out in their own lives onto the lives of their own children. And when their children don't share the same level of drive and enthusiasm, the parents fail to understand why. My personal experience has been that unless the goal truly resonates with that person, the level of drive, desire, and determination will never be as great.
- It's your vision. You don't have to seek the approval of others. This is where you want to go.
- It's okay to change course. We are not doomed to the first path that we choose. We can abandon the goal we set, if there's good reason to do so. We can re-define the goal itself, or change the way we approach it. Initially we may have foggy notions and ideas. We have difficulty expressing ourselves, or putting our vision into words. But with practice, our ideas become clearer, and in which case, we can revise our written goals;
- Don't allow inertia, fear, laziness or the comfort zone stop you from working towards what's meaningful to you. The journey will not be easy. Compromises and sacrifices will arise. That's part and parcel of the process. Invest the effort and resources into planning and execution. It will yield great dividends.

> ### Set goals based on what you want, not what you *don't* want
>
> The latter cannot be made in to a goal, as it doesn't direct you to a *destination*. It may get you away from the starting line, but you are clueless on where to go next. If you go on the basis of what you don't want, you confuse your mind, as the mind will perpetually be left asking "what else **don't** you want?". The mind will have a list of "don't wants" but no specific destination to head towards. As a result you will lead a clueless life that is devoid of direction. Begin with the premise of what you *want* as the destination, as it helps keep your eyes fixed on a definite finish line. Every person who is successful in his field will have set goals about what they want.
>
> Yo-Yo Ma didn't become a world class cellist by going through a process of elimination. It's unlikely he had said to himself, "I'm not cut out to be a world class race car driver or a world class tennis player. Therefore I think I shall be a world class cellist instead." He would have the goal of being a world class cellist firmly in his mind from the outset. And all his time effort and energies were then focused on achieving this one single objective.

Practice makes perfect

Setting goals does not become "easier" when you're an adult. On the contrary, the task gets harder over time, as the challenges will become more complex. Therefore begin learning the art of setting goals as early as possible. With the advantage of having more practice, one would become much better and effective in the art, and this will give a tremendous advantage in adulthood.

If you look around, you will notice many people (including our family member, friends, and colleagues) go about their lives without setting any real definite life goals. Yes, they make plans for the next vacation, where they want to go for lunch or their next social gathering. Superficial plans, but not those that affect their long range direction in life. It is as if they live from day to day, content to just allow life to take them where it wishes, rather than the other way around. If you live life seeing where it takes you, then don't be disappointed if it doesn't take you where *you* want to go.

Start by setting simple easy goals. Like reading a number of books by a certain period of time. Or running a certain distance within a week. Or doing the household chores that you've been putting off for the longest time. Or taking the effort to reach out and speak to a friend or family member whom you've not spoken to for a while.

What's important to take away from these situations is the experience of accomplishment. How it feels, and what is needed emotionally, physically and intellectually to carry out the tasks, step-by-step until the goal is eventually achieved. Feel the emotional "high" and the satisfaction and completion that the event gives you. From there, move on to bigger and more complex goals.

As goals are referenced to a time-frame, they can be categorised according the amount of time it takes to reach it. So, for ease of reference, the terms long-term, mid-term and short-term goals are often used. They are not used only in work or academic related activities, but in almost all aspects of life.

Don't let the planning the minor details paralyse you from starting. Some planning is good, but we can't plan for every contingency in life. So just adapt and be flexible with whatever that comes about.

I like to use the analogy of a person embarking on a long distance trip by car. The traveller would carry out the basic preparations e.g. packing his luggage and ensure he has his passport, and that the car is in reasonable state of repair. The traveller definitely cannot see the destination from the point of departure but he knows with certainty that his destination is there. And he starts driving. All he sees is the

the couple of kilometers in front of him, or a couple of hundred meters if the weather is bad. But by and by, he will eventually reach his destination.

The traveller doesn't change course part way through the journey, just because he thinks that he's not making any progress or he's taking too long to reach the destination. He perseveres in his efforts, knowing that he will eventually arrive. Along the way, he will see milestones that tell him how far he has progressed. Similarly he will adjust his course for any road obstructions, pot holes and traffic congestion that he may encounter during the joinery.

So in the same way, we must have a definite goal. We go on with our life, with this goal in mind, and intent on working towards it. And most essentially, knowing that its completion is already at hand, and waiting for us to arrive at it!

<u>An exercise in goal-setting</u>

The next time that you're planning for a vacation overseas, use it as a simple exercise of goal-setting.

Firstly, have a mental image of the travel destination that you desire. Develop a detailed mental image of the destination, of the people, surroundings, activities and food. If necessary get references to help you create a better mental image. For instance, get a picture of a famous landmark that the desired destination has.

Now break the planning into smaller steps, such as booking the hotel rooms and the air tickets, purchasing the travel insurance, getting your flu shots, packing your clothes and changing money to the local currency.

Set a deadline by which each and every component of the travel plan are to be completed. Prioritise the various sub-tasks in order of their importance. In this case, plan and coordinate the flight and hotel accommodations, to ensure that at the very least you are able to get there and back and you will have a roof over your heads whilst you're there.

Carry out the remaining sub-tasks until they are all completed.

Once you are there, go to the spot where the picture of the landmark was taken, and take a picture of the landmark yourself. Even better, take a picture **with** the landmark. Now you will see that it is possible to manifest into reality what was previously merely an idea resident in your mind.

Multiple reasons - which do we have our eyes on?

We may have a multitude of reasons for the goal we set, and unless we are conscious of these (potentially conflicting) reasons, we may not experience the satisfaction we seek when we accomplish it. The differing reasons may (i) necessitate different approaches to arriving at the same goal, and (ii) different parameters by which we define success in that endeavour. We may reach the same goal, but the end-state will look different depending on which reason we had chosen to focus on.

Let's take the example of two individuals who set a goal to take up and complete a postgraduate course. One individual's reason for taking up the course is to secure a post-grad qualification to improve his résumé whereas the other individual's purpose is to improve his understanding of the subjects offered in the course syllabus.

Depending on the reasons, the way that the two individuals may go about studying (in terms of allocation of resources, etc.) and appreciating the subjects may be vastly different. The former may be more interested in finding out how to get best grades, and may not be interested to go beyond the course materials. This individual's actions will be primed towards getting the best grade possible. Whereas the latter may, out of his interest in the subject matter, ask questions on issues that are not even in the course syllabus. This is, of course, not to suggest that the latter is not interested in his grades, or the certificate. However his primary focus, due to the reason for which he has set this goal, is to have a better understanding of the subject matter; rather than just his grades and the certificate per se. Both students will also see 'effectiveness' and 'efficiency' differently. The first would see effectiveness and efficiency as getting to the end point by the fastest way and with the least resources. On the other hand, the individual who is taking on the course purely out of the love for the subject may not even consider efficiency as an objective. He will take as much time and resources as is needed to fully understand and master the subject.

Therefore understanding the presence of multiple (and possibly competing) reasons allow us make better informed decisions and compromises. By making a conscious and informed decision, we control the outcome and are better able to deal with the consequences of our decision. It is inevitable that compromises have to be made in the pursuit of any goals. However it's one thing to make a compromise knowingly, and another to compromise in ignorance.

Visualising your ideal life

Create a vision of your life. If you were not limited by the lack of funds, limiting beliefs, objections and practical limitations, how would you see yourself to be now? What would you be doing for leisure? How would contribute to others? Spiritually? How would you feel about this way of life? It is my view that this is what your inner vision of what life truly is. And that's what you will need to work towards. The vision of your ideal life will also affect you emotionally in a good way, helping you to persist in your efforts to make your vision to reality.

We are likely to have different views of what our ideal life is when we are children, adolescents, adults and in our old age. They may not, and are unlikely, to be the same. Nonetheless we may have principles or convictions of how our life is to be lived regardless of age and circumstance.

For instance, if your mantra is to be the very best that you can in all you do, this principle will flesh itself out in your work life, social life and personal life. The things that you may do in each aspect of your life may differ, but you will do your best in all of it. On the other hand, if your principle is to have a good time in everything that you do, this can also manifest in your daily activities.

Make being the best you can be a goal

Make it a life goal to do your very best in everything that you do. Instill the desire to be your best into every other goal that you may set. This ensures that you will get the very best results in everything you do. For the quality of your work tells people who you are as a person. Perform your work as if to tell the world through your products and services, the person that you are, and what are your values, philosophies and standards. And your work **does** tell the people around you all these things whether you choose to believe it or not.

We can often assess a person's character attitude and personality accurately from the type of work that he or she produces. The condition of his workplace. His physical appearance, how he carries himself, and his living conditions. If he or she is neat and organised, that person is likely to be neat and organised in his thoughts. If he is slovenly, then it's quite likely that his thought processes will also be the same too.

Look at your work objectively from time to time. How would you assess it, if it were someone else's work. Would you think it is excellent, merely average, or mediocre? Can you honestly say that you could have done better? So be the best in all that you can do.

Having said that, don't allow your ego get in the way, and let yourself to be attached to the end result. Do not be attached to your mental image of how your actions will help others, or that it should "help" them in only the way you perceive it to. Similarly don't be fixated with how others will perceive your efforts, what your efforts' influence will ultimately be, or how your efforts will be accepted. Just perform the task with the pure sincerity and earnestness of your deepest spirit, and release it to the world. Let God determine the rest. I believe that by doing so, we will create our best works every single time.

Live your own life goals

And by this, I am referring to two things. Firstly, never live another's person's life goal. Never let another person set your life goals for you. No matter how good or noble their intentions may be. Whilst their suggestions may be useful guides, however you must ultimately decide what *you* want to do. Otherwise accepting the life goals that others have set for you, or adopting the goals of others as your own often leads to you feeling frustrated and unhappy. Since they are extrinsic factors, you will lack the much needed commitment and drive to pursue them wholeheartedly.

We frequently see this happening when parents want impose their will on their children to join a certain profession. It could be an occupation that the parent himself wanted to pursue, but was denied the opportunity. Or it may be that the parent considers that occupation is prestigious, or will make lots of money. So they direct their child's development towards that profession without having any regard to whether this chosen field is indeed consistent with the child's abilities or if the child even has the aptitude to that line of work.

> Secondly, don't live your life vicariously either. Whether through your friends, your children or through the television. "Reality TV" is perhaps one of life's greatest oxymoron. Why are we experiencing life through the trials and tribulations of others? We go through every stage of life but only once, so be fully engaged in it. Don't just be a spectator, be an active life participant!

Time - our most valuable yet overlooked resource

Time. It is the one single resource that the world's richest man and the world's poorest beggar have in equal measure. The most expensive watch and the cheapest watch that you can ever find have exactly the same of number of digits on its face - 1 to 12. The rich and powerful are not accorded any more time than the others by reason of their position or their wealth.

When the short hand goes around the face twice, it means a day has passed, both for the wealthy and the poor. The crucial difference lies in how the poor and the rich man use their time. The wealthy and successful are greatly aware of how precious time is, and use it very carefully and productively. Whereas those who are not treat it as an abundant never-ending supply.

Energy can be recovered. Our worldly possessions, if lost, can be replaced. But the time that we have is priceless, limited in quantity and is never replenish-able. All the money in the world won't buy you back a single second once it is passed.

Lack of time is an oft-cited reason why things don't get accomplished. But you don't find time to do something, you make time to do it. Life will pass us by, whether we spend it working all the time, or just sitting on the living room couch watching TV. Often you will find that we sit around and allow time to be frittered away wastefully.

To make the time you spend worthwhile, decide what is truly valuable to you. Then do it. There will *always* time to do what needs to be done. It's simply of a matter of being disciplined, planning, and taking control of the time you have.

Time adheres strictly to the principle of opportunity cost. Time used for one activity willl be at the expense of another. So you have to make time i.e. setting aside time intended for one activity to be used for another. Life will always have chores that "need to be done". But if it's important to you, then it's definitely worth investing time in it. Look at it as a short-term pain for a long-term gain.

Of course, it's one thing to be wasteful, and another being too rigid with time management. We each need to find the balance of what works for us. There is a time for work and labour. There's also a time to sit back, and experience life. **Life can just as easily pass us by when we are too busy working as when we just sit and do nothing.** It's about prioritising. Perhaps time allocation should be on the basis of what gives you the most enjoyment in life - the intrinsic resonance - given the circumstances at that point in time of your life.

"Long-term goals" vs "Long-time goals"

We must be careful when we use the phrase "long-term goal". Do we mean a project that will require months or possibly years to complete? Or is it a project that will be undertaken "some time in the future" or if certain conditions are met. If it is the latter, I suggest using another term for it, such as "long-time goal". This is so that we can distinguish between a project that takes a long time to complete, from a project that is undertaken "some time in the future". It's important to distinguish between the two because long-time goals are very unlikely (if ever) to be carried out, let alone achieved since there's no specific deadline by which it starts and when it ends. It's merely wishful thinking or a pipe dream.

If you truly desire a goal, **anytime** is a great time to start. Even today! The earlier you start off on a long-time goal, the sooner you can enjoy the fruits of its completion. This may be so even if the goal is dependent on certain conditions being met, it is no longer a long-time goal but a long-term goal. You know it will happen as soon as the conditions are met. You just work need to work at meeting those conditions.

Procrastination

Perhaps this experience may sound familiar to you. Let's say as you're heading towards your office, you decide that you will clear up your "In" tray which has started to stack with correspondence.

However upon arriving at the office, you are immediately beset upon by urgent e-mails, phone calls from customers, paperwork, requests from colleagues for help. The day is filled up with to-ing and fro-ing, and the end of it, you realise that your appointed task for the day is nowhere close to being started, let alone completed. Clearing your "In" tray ends up on the back burner again. But the process repeats itself again the next day. With each passing day, the mound of papers in your tray looms ever higher. Then one day you miss a deadline because you didn't see the memo which was buried underneath the mound of papers on the tray. And you wonder why your life involves running from one urgent crisis to another.

This can happen with even simple and mundane tasks too, such as household chores. For instance, tidying the room or doing the laundry during the weekend. Somehow there will always be a more pressing task that will come along that will take you away from your intended task. This may still be the case even if there aren't any "urgent" issues that need your immediate attention. Somehow you'd still prefer to do anything rather than starting on the intended task.

If we put our foot down and consciously decide how much time should be allocated for our daily activities, life becomes more meaningful. We achieve and experience more out of life.

> ### Procrastination - are we being too optimistic of our future abilities?
>
> When we put off important tasks to a later date, we believe that our future self will have the requisite discipline, resolve and time to do what we are unable to do now. But the truth is, why would our future self be any different from our present self if we don't fundamentally alter who we are now?
>
> Pushing tasks till a later date merely ensures that this trend will perpetuate. If we don't change now, what will make the change easier to accomplish in the future?
>
> Hence (1) don't put off to tomorrow what can be done today. You will *still* procrastinate when tomorrow comes; and (2) redouble your efforts so that the deadlines remain realistically attainable.

'Busy' does not always equate to being effective

Do you know people who are constantly busy? They come into the office and are a flurry of activity. They're constantly moving around the office in a hurry and seem to be doing a lot of things. Yet 'busy-ness' is not the same as being productive. These people major in minor things.

Be a major in major things. Learn to work on the important tasks for a greater positive impact on your quality of life. Learn to do them well. Whether at work or at home. Do this and life will reward you with experiences that far surpass what the ordinary person would experience.

Learn to allocate time to each daily, monthly and annual tasks. Be realistic about your abilities and how much time you need. Don't allocate more time than is necessary to complete any task, as this means you will have less time for others. But more often than not, we usually underestimate the amount of time needed, and end up feeling rushed and stressed. As a result, the task is completed unsatisfactorily, if at all.

Once a task is completed, review your actions and see if you could have been faster in doing it without compromising the quality of your work. Consistently seek ways to improve the way in which you perform and explore if a different method could be used to save time. Then you can begin to shorten the time complete it.

Always store your implements, books and tools for the tasks at hand in an organised easy to find manner. This saves time having to stop what you're doing, disrupting your line of thought and go around hunting for the necessary tool.

Systemise. If the task is routine or process-driven, it is a good opportunity to systemise it. Discover ways to break the task down to a step-by-step process as this helps to increase efficiency and yield consistent results. See if any task can be outsourced, or if it can be done together with other tasks or activities. For instance, going to the post office whilst grocery shopping. Plan the route and activities so that they flow smoothly, and reduce the commuting or waiting time. Take any free time or time spent waiting as an opportunity to improve yourself. Read a book or listen instead of opting to just walk aimlessly around a shopping mall, watching TV or playing a video game. Every little bit counts.

> **Reflections on Time**
> * In a wider sense, "time" is a mental construct. It is a measurement man has created to have a reference point to events that have already occurred, is happening now or will take place.

- In that sense, time is used to create a distinction between events occurring right <u>now</u> and those that are not.

- Other than this mental construct, events just happen.

- Contingent "future" events <u>always</u> remain speculative. There are no certainty that forecasted events <u>will</u> indeed take place. Nothing is certain <u>until</u> it takes place in the now.

- In contrast, the "time" we have as individuals (to be precise, our life span) is finite. We will die one day. When that day will arrive is uncertain.

- From that personal perspective, "time" is a limited resource and very precious. We can earn money to buy our worldly possessions. But no amount of money buys us a longer life.

- Once past, events in life cannot be re-wound as in a movie and re-lived again. Whilst we can do the same activity at the same place and with the same people, it will be in a distinctly different stage of our life.

- 'Time' as a resource will pass regardless of whether we use it, or how we use it. Unlike other resources which can be set aside in reserve until it is allocated for a purpose, time will pass whether we are busy in the office, or lazing in front of the TV. It cannot be turned on and off like a light switch. Hence it must be used *intelligently* and *purposefully* to achieve the most out of your life and your life experience.

- Focus on what you do with *life*, rather than what you do with time.

- Do everything with a purpose. Even at leisure. Don't be content to do things just to "pass time". You do it for a reason, and time just happens to pass as you're doing it,

- Time alone cannot guarantee success. For instance, we have a weak volley in our tennis game. But we find it tedious to practise our approach shots, running from the baseline to the net is just too much work. So we focus on our forehand during practice sessions instead. Just doing this and thinking "give it time, and my volley will improve" won't get us a better volley.
- Therein lies the other aspect of time as a resource. It **must** be allocated to the activity that takes us to achieving our desired goal. If it means less time potato-couching in front of the TV and more time on the tennis court, then time must be allocated accordingly.
- Using our time on what we are **already** doing now won't give us a different life that what we are currently experiencing. We need to take on new activities in place of, or in addition to what we are currently doing.
- Money cannot buy back our personal time. Every present moment that goes, goes away forever. It may remain as a memory, but it cannot be re-used.
- Therefore use time to fully maximise the good emotions and experiences in life. There is no right or wrong way to experience life. We are all different. Go with what suits you.

Time's relevance to success

Time by itself has not bearing to whether you can attain success or not. I want to use the example of the pot of coffee. In order to successfully brew a pot of coffee, we must gather all the necessary ingredients beforehand: coffee powder, sugar, hot water and milk. How soon the steaming pot of coffee can materialise depends on how much time you need to get the ingredients together. If they are all readily available, it may take less than five minutes. If you need to boil the hot water, it may take perhaps ten minutes. If you've run out of coffee powder, then it will take as much time as you will need to get to the store to get some. If the store's closed, then you'd need to wait a whole lot longer to get the pot of coffee. Or if you get distracted as you are driving to the store to get the coffee powder, and end up at another destination, then it will take longer for the pot of coffee to materialise too.

From this example, we can conclude that time is merely a *consequence* of the process. Success requires only so much time as you need to get all the necessary ingredients together. Time passes as we get all the ingredients together. Time by itself does not improve the chances of success. It is merely a measure of how long it takes for all ingredients of the goal to fall into place.

Consequently how soon we can achieve success in any of our endeavours depend largely on **how fast we can bring the necessary ingredients together**. You may have heard people using the phrase "give it some time". Success will not happen if all the necessary ingredients are not present, no matter how much time you give it! Unless you actively working on bringing the necessary ingredients together, merely "giving it some time" gets you nowhere. Secondly, believing that over time by just "working" on ingredients that you already have, without taking any effort on getting the *remaining* ingredients, will not get you anywhere closer to your goal either. Stirring a pot of hot water, no matter how diligently or how long, without any coffee powder does not a pot of coffee make. Thirdly, if any of the elements involves a repetitive process, just going through the motions without actually being effective will not bring the elements closer to a state of completion. Be conscious and in the present moment when you execute the process.

> **The ingredients to success**
>
> It is important to understand that the ingredients may not come sequentially or in the order that you will expect it to. Secondly, they may sometimes come from sources that we least expect. It's therefore important to keep our eyes and ears opened for these bits of information and windows of opportunities that will bring us closer to achieving out goals. It is as if once we have defined the end goal, our mind will subconsciously filter all incoming data (regardless of its source) for the ones that matter.

Patience

What does "patience" mean to you? We often associate this word with the act of simply allowing time to pass. I would like to proffer an alternative view: Patience means accepting that success will only take place when all the elements necessary for success are in place, and **accepting** the time needed for the elements to fall into place. We can't will success to take place before then. That would be like digging up a seed we have planted in the ground every few days to see if it's growing. Perhaps the underlying foundation to patience is faith - to believe that things will turn out fine in the end. We water the plant, and fertilise the soil, and trusting God will take care of the rest. We don't over-water or put in more fertiliser than is necessary in the belief that this would speed the process up. That would be impatience. We allow the seed such time as it needs with the proper nutrition to break through the ground and grow.

So in the same way, whilst we may have done all that we can to get the ingredients of success together, we must allow the necessary amount of time to pass for the ingredients to fall into place.

Keeping a Journal

The act of writing puts your thoughts into a tangible form, something that you see and physically touch. For once, you are able to hold your thoughts in your very hands. The feeling is deeply satisfying.

Putting your personal thoughts down on paper may feel unnatural initially However this step is important as it records your important thoughts, and keep them organised so that you can return to them later on. Your journal will help you see how your life perceptions and beliefs may have changed over time.

Have a notebook nearby so that you can jot down your thoughts. Don't be lazy. Do it. Get a notebook that that is easy to carry around, and something that feels "special" and with which you can establish a connection with; because this is where you are going to pen down your thoughts, feelings and life experiences and feelings. An electronic tablet works great too. Just remember to back up all the contents from time to time!

You can write it in as much detail as you want, or jot your thoughts down in point form. Adopt a method that feels comfortable to you, but always in a way so that it's understandable to you. Also, if you're writing it in point form, remember what the key words and short forms mean. Because these words may not bear the same meaning to you in the future, as it does now! As I said at the beginning of this book, words may convey different emotions and meanings at different periods of our lives.

Be ready to catch your best ideas!

I have often had my most profound and insightful ideas and thoughts in the shower. Or even when I'm doing laps in the pool. Perhaps water has a way of inspiring our minds. So don't discount the bathroom as a place to think and reflect, too! Keep a notebook or pen and paper nearby to jot down your lightbulb moments. Write it down as soon as it strikes, as they often elude us after we finish our shower.

Conclusion

Goal-setting, as we have seen, is the glue that connects our ideas and thoughts to the action we need to take for our ideas to take form. Investing the time to set our goals before starting pays great dividends by ensuring that our actions are coherent, effective and efficient.

We experience greater levels of happiness and excitement when working towards than after we have attained success. This is an interesting anomaly. Perhaps you may be under the impression that we will experience greater levels of emotions once we have achieved what we set out to do. Along the way, we visualise all the good feelings that will come with the completion of the project. We feel happier and more excited as we check off the sub-goals and tasks in our written plan one by one.

As we get closer to the completion of the project, the anticipation grows. Excitement mounts. And the day finally arrives. We will feel a sense of accomplishment and satisfaction. And perhaps a sense of peace But the good emotions which we experience immediately after success does not last. The emotions taper off. At times, very drastically. Soon our mind becomes restless. We turn our attention towards the horizon and the next goal. Pretty soon we find ourselves working on a new project.

Does it mean we are easily dissatisfied? Not at all. I proffer an alternative viewpoint. For each journey that we undertake, we avail ourselves to opportunities to learn, and gain experience and wisdom. And each journey brings to us anew all the emotions that come with expanding our abilities, discovering and exploring new mental and physical frontiers.

We have covered three of the primary principles. In the next chapter we talk about the final principle, namely the need to take action. This is where our attitudes and goals move from the realm of pure potentiality and transform themselves into reality.

PART 4

Action

Taking action is the fourth essential principle necessary to consistently achieve success in life. Applying the the earlier three principles without action is like building a castle in the air. Making your dreams come true requires you to get up and do things. It can't be delegated to someone else. Taking action can be broken down into two essential components: you have to start, and you have to persist.

The case for action

It's through our actions that we tell the world about our understanding and interpretation of the knowledge we possess; and by our actions and the service we render to others, we tell the world who we are and what we stand for. We tell ourselves and the people around us that the faith, values and beliefs we have in our hearts and minds also hold true in our actions. We show to ourselves and unto others that we say can indeed be done, and we are good for our words.

Without action, our new positive attitude and confidence exist purely as thought form. It is only when we take action do we put our new found positive self-belief and confidence to the test. For instance, you can't just say "I'm a changed man". You may be a happier person now in your thoughts but if don't show it in how you

111

behave, how you do things and relate to others, you won't convince anyone, including yourself.

Action puts our ideas and dreams into something tangible that we can see and touch. It brings us closer to our goal. Without action, we will forever remain on this side of the divide, and our goals on the other, forever out of our reach as if we never had them in the first place.

Action begins a journey. We won't learn much if we remain sitting on the couch facing the same four walls of our living room day in, day out. Nor will we meet new people, or increase the chance of coming across opportunities this way. People and opportunities don't just make their way into our living room and present themselves to us. We go out and meet them.

Fear often holds us back from realising our dreams. The longer you allow fear to to hold you back, the further your dreams are pushed back. We overcome our greatest fears and doubt by confronting and overcoming them. We stare down our fears and doubts. Telling them to go to the furthest reaches of our minds, never to shackle us with limitations again. Take action now, for otherwise the world is a poorer place without your ideas and dreams seeing light of day. It's only when we put action to our words that we see how we truly react to pressure, adversity, disappointment and pain. We will see all the areas in which we are strong, and those that need strengthening. We cultivate confidence, resilience, courage and determination through action. These virtues are a necessary consequence, and a by-product of action. They cannot be learnt academically.

When we put things into motion, we increase our wealth of information and experience thereby helping us to become wiser. Wisdom can't be learnt through books. On the contrary, the experience and wisdom we gather in our life journey help give meaning to the words in books. Which is why re-reading books allow us to "see" things that we didn't notice during the previous readings.

Getting Started

Live life for all it's worth. Don't hesitate because of (a) how it might look to others, (b) what others will think of you, or (c) it's not the "right thing" to do. So long as what you intend to do it does not harm others - and a large percentage of the activities that we contemplate won't - why are you holding yourself back? It is the ego, and our limiting thought processes that are restraining us from our true potential.

Of course, by living our life to the fullest doesn't mean that we have a valid excuse to break the law! But I am sure that a vast majority of the things we desire to do are neither immoral nor illegal. Yet we we hold ourselves back with "excuses" that are without any rational basis.

Remember that if you tarry too long, there may come a time in your life when our goals will be physically impossible to do, or can no longer be achieved due to change of circumstances. Once that window of opportunity is closed, we may live to regret that lost opportunity. The ideal situation would be never to have to lie at our death bed, and wishing that we had more time to do the things we had put off. Wouldn't it be great if we could, at that point in time, look back and know that we had experienced all the very best and finest life had to offer?

Pluck up the courage and take the plunge! Make it a purpose in life, at least once a year, to achieve one major goal that you've always wanted to. It might be learning a new skill, a sport, or even taking on a new vocation. Do it and cross it out in your checklist of to-do's. Also do try a novel activity or experience once a month.

What holds us back

Even after we have adopted the right attitude, are clear about the goal we set and why we want achieve that goal, we may still resist starting. A change in mindset as well as goal-setting are essentially internally-driven processes. However it's when we take action that external factors beyond our control are involved.

Most goals will require changes, in one way or another. A goal may entail changes to our life routines or the way we do things. This in turn affects our family members, friends, the people we come into contact with, and even the community that we are in. As a result of the far-reaching implications of these changes, we experience fear and uncertainty about the changes the goal entails. It's as if the mind places the pro's and con's of goal, and the pro's and con's of remaining status quo at opposing ends of a weighing scale.

Change will not take place if the perceived "pain" or inconvenience associated with the process, or the consequence, of change as well as the benefits of remaining status quo outweigh the benefits resulting from the change. Therefore in order to tip the scales in favour of taking action on the goal, we have to (i) increase the benefits from the change, (ii) reduce the pain or discomfort associated with the process or the consequence of the change.

Here are some suggestions:

1) Prepare the way. Try eliminating the pain of starting, where possible, one by one so that the discomfort of starting is minimal. For instance, you can adjust your schedules and routines to accommodate the impending change. You can also share your plans for the future with the people who will be affected by the change, so as to prepare them for what's about to come.

   Another benefit of sharing your plans and goals with others is that you show that you care for them and have taken *their* routines and lifestyle into consideration. In this way, you overcome some of the resistance that others may initially put up when you take action, and they may become more supportive of your efforts.

2) Ease yourself into the start. In situations where it's possible to implement the change gradually, do so rather than attempt it all at once. These are usually goals that affect more than one aspect of our life. By addressing one constituent at a time, you make the discomfort of change more tolerable. Before you know it, you would have eased into the new routines and the changes would have become a part of your life.

3) Tip the scale in favour of change. Where it's not possible to have a experience the benefits of a change beforehand, accentuate the pains of remaining status quo. By doing so, the benefits of the change is magnified and becomes more tangible. Consequently we create a greater incentive to implement the change.

Potentiality

Every day is a whole new vista of potentiality, of possibilities and opportunities ripe for the picking. For every "no" you encounter on the way to success, know that there is a "yes" just around the corner. We need only go about our affairs quietly, and with a heart full of optimism and faith of the opportunities lying before us.

Every day is a chance at (1) doing more, (2) at doing better and (3) at doing something new altogether. Today is not like the day before. As today comes to a end, tomorrow is a new day with all the potential opportunities and possibilities reset to 'full' again. Everything is different. The combination of people, events, circumstances and even the environment are different. These variations throw up an infinite range of possibilities. It's for us to take advantage of these variations and make the very best of it.

Every day that you wake up and are still alive, is an opportunity to begin the journey to radically change your life. Every single day that you tarry, is another opportunity wasted. And the window of opportunity closes ever so slightly.

Consequences of our action or inaction

The Ripple Effect

Just like a pebble hitting the surface of a calm pond, your actions (whether good or bad) will also ripple out and affect other areas of your life. The consequences of your actions will frequently affect areas of your life that you least expect it to.

For instance, a person who fails to take care of his body may see that his lack of fitness and energy affect his performance at work. This in turn impacts his chances of promotion and wage increments. Likewise this may also affect his relationships with his family and friends as he has limited energy for social activities. Conversely by taking more care of his health will result in an improvement in both his working and social life. He will also experience an improvement in the overall quality of life, just because of one positive change in his life.

So it is wise to choose your decisions and actions carefully. Know that the conscious decision to act in the general good will have a positive ripple out effect. And that's a good thing to have!

> "Knowledge without action is useless. Action without knowledge is dangerous." - Confuscius

Now that you've decided to embark on the journey of personal change, you might realise that you don't have much information on how to get started. So let's consider the process of learning and beliefs we may have about this process.

Attitude towards Learning

What's your attitude towards learning? Do you have a voice in your head that says "I know that" or "I don't need to learn that" whenever someone tries to give you some advice. If this attitude has thus served you well far not, perhaps a change of attitude is in order. Adopt the attitude that you are an empty vessel, waiting for information to be "poured" into you.

Be ready to accept the advice that is proffered at face value for the moment, without any preconceived notions. Then objectively evaluate the information later to see if what is said is true or acceptable and can be applied to improve your life. It is only when we acquire more information and knowledge that the options and choices open up for us.

All the information that was, is, and ever shall be is already in existence. It is never created. It has always been present, waiting for us to "discover" it.

For instance, electricity has always existed even though mankind only become aware of its existence in the 1600s. We are limited to five physical senses and we need to accept that there are things that exist beyond what we can perceive with these five simple, rudimentary senses. Just because these things can't be perceived does not mean that they don't exist. As such we need to trust and believe that there is a greater Divine Intelligence at work.

We need only tap into the Divine Intelligence for the answers to our questions. Therefore whenever you are confounded by a problem, don't become anxious or fretful. But be confident that you just need to work towards the general direction of the solution. And the solution will reveal itself to you. The solution may not however reveal itself in the way or in the place that we seek it. And that's why it's always good to keep an open mind, ear and eye to what is happening in the world.

Beliefs about Learning

Two predominant beliefs that we have with regard to learning. Firstly, we believe that learning only occurs within a formal environment or in the form of "formal" education. We may believe that if we have been denied an opportunity to pursue a formal education, or if we did not complete our course of formal education, we are at a severe disadvantage. The second belief may be that we can stop learning as soon as we leave school. We have nothing more to learn outside the realm of the classroom.

I invite you to consider the alternative view.

Lessons outside the classroom

If you did not have the opportunity to have any formal education, or your formal education is incomplete, or you did not do well in school; this is not an insurmountable obstacle. It does not mean you don't have any opportunity to learn. Information and knowledge can be acquired in as many ways as our imagination can come up with, so long as there is a desire within us to acquire it. Formal education is purely a process by which lessons are imparted. It does not mean that if you don't have access to textbooks or a teacher, education is inaccessible to you.

Life's Lessons

Life is comprised of thousands upon thousands of little lessons as we go along. Unfortunately the school of hard knocks does not organise its lessons appropriate to our age or level of experience. You might encounter an advanced class in relationships and be faced with a 101 class in another life subject. We can't pick and choose these lessons. And we can't opt out!

We may know, or heard stories of children whose parents may have abandoned them or whose parents passed away whilst they were still young. These children had to fend for themselves, sometimes having to work at a very tender age to support themselves and their siblings. This is an instance of individuals being thrown into an advanced "class" of the school of hard knocks. Kids who would, in usual circumstances, be playing with other children of their age are forced to enter into a world beyond their age and experience. At times like these, life seems a cruel teacher under these circumstances. Yet in spite of this, many have gone on to achieve great things. It all lies in how we view our life circumstances, and deal with them. The better we are at learning life's lessons, and more adept we become in applying these lessons, the further ahead we get in the class.

We place much value on "formal education"; the process of learning in a structured classroom environment replete with course materials, tutors, assignments and tests. Whilst important, and arguably one of the most effective way of imparting knowledge, we must realise that a classroom is just the means human beings use to relay their thoughts, ideas and lessons learnt in the course of life. The fact that we derive most of our education in school does not make us "better" educated or cause to place a lower value to lessons learnt outside the classroom.

Ultimately our true education comes from applying the ideas and principles in real life, in whatever manner we may have learnt them. It means putting what we've learnt into practice. No matter how many accounts of other people's experience we may read, it will never comprehensively prepare us for our *own* life and it will *never* replace the need to do it ourselves.

Our natural tendency is to embark on the new area with our existing skill sets, closing off our minds to new ideas and techniques. To cite an extreme example, it's like saying that your skills in roller blading will be useful when you take up cooking! Since the new activity involves entirely different skills and abilities, it require learning (or re-learning) skills in order to become competent in the new activity.

Life's lessons will come in different ways and forms. Do not be concerned with the "teacher", which may appear in the form of a thing, an event or a life situation. Instead be more concerned about the lesson or the message that is being imparted.

Learning is a continuous process

If you have completed your formal education, it does not mean that the learning process stops. In truth, what we learn in the classroom represents but only a minuscule portion of all the things life can teach us! Let's consider another extreme example. At the age of 8 years, a child decides that he has learnt enough by then to get him through life. After all, he would have mastered his alphabets and possessed a rudimentary grasp of mathematics. Hence he is of the view that there is nothing more that formal education can possibly teach him. Of course, no reasonable parent will agree with that child's point of view. There is so much more to learn and explore; the child, with his limited perspective of the world, is unable to appreciate this.

With that example in mind, on what basis then can we determine that 21 will be the right cut-off point? Or perhaps when we obtain our university degree? Or when we get a job? Or when we are married and have kids? Or could it be that we will continue to learn, for so long as we have (or create) the opportunity to learn? So whenever we feel that there's nothing more to learn, we remind ourselves that we may just be like that 8-year old child...

Using existing vs new knowledge

Whenever we take up a new activity, work or a sport, our natural reaction is to stay to the tried and true, namely to use whatever knowledge and experience that we currently have, and apply it to the new enterprise. We may have an unconscious belief that what worked previously will work again. However this belief might limit our ability to reach our fullest potential.

I think that keeping an a really open, clear and non-judgmental mind is crucial as it allows us to see if the knowledge and experience that we currently have is useful, and at the same time enable us to learn new skills, gain new knowledge and experience. With an open and receptive mind we discern ways in which our existing knowledge may be adapted and/or where new methods may be improved. It's having the benefit of the beginner's mind - where there are many possibilities.

Gathering information

Be willing to read. Not just on trivialities but academic subjects as well. All of man's achievements and progress have been premised on his ability to to relay knowledge and information to his fellow man and the future generations. Take the time to read, and see what the vast wealth of stored knowledge has to offer. You can be quite certain that the issues you are facing have at one time or another been encountered by another human being. So don't reinvent the wheel. See if others have succeeded where you have failed. Or if they have failed, see what they have done so as to avoid their fate. Be prepared to ask for directions to get anywhere in life as we don't have the answers to everything.

One of the best, comprehensive and efficient source of information available to us is the Internet. Whilst not *always* reliable, it will almost always point you in the right direction to where you may find what you're looking for. Talking to the right people works, too. This often means talking to people who are outside our normal circle of acquaintances. Don't be shy about it. This, too, is part of the learning process. It is a skill that once learned will reap great befits in your future endeavours.

Reading effectively

When reading a non-fiction book with a view to self-improvement, or to gather knowledge or learn a new skill, do it actively rather than in a passive manner. If it's done in the latter fashion, its quite likely you are going through the motions and not fully absorbing what is being read. You could find yourself just seeing the words and not understanding the sentences. Or you're just looking at a page full of words but your mind is really somewhere else. If this is happening, then you are just wasting your time. This may happen for several reasons. You may be preoccupied with other matters. Or you might just be tired. It would be better to approach it again when you're fresh and able to focus better.

For subject matters that are dry and require a considerable effort to understand, you need to clearly define the information you are seeking before commencing, so that the reading process has specific objectives. With these objectives in mind, you are able go to through the text specifically seeking the information you need. By reading actively, you are also able to quickly assess if the book is shedding any light on the topic that you are researching on.

To make reading a truly worthwhile endeavour, take time to analyse and reflect on what is being said. If possible, it may help to underline and make notes beside the paragraphs that have made an impact on you. Especially if the subject matter requires you to reflect further, or if it's something that you can't put into practice immediately.

As a matter of personal practice, I try to take away at least ten new points from every non-fiction book that I read. By "new" I am referring to points that I have not come across in other materials. This habit it forces me to read the book actively, and to be on the look out for these new points. I will write these points down in pencil in the blank pages at the back of book so that it's easier to retrieve them without having to re-read the entire book again.

With the advent of the electronic book, highlighting bookmarking and searching for key words has become much easier and efficient. Nevertheless penning down you're thoughts is one of the simplest and fastest ways by which thoughts can be manifested into reality. Never underestimate the power and the reach of the written thought.

Learning to ask a better question

This is an important life skill. It goes like this: ask vague and fuzzy questions, and you will get vague and fuzzy answers. The answer will likely not be what you want to hear, and it would certainly not make the situation any clearer than before you asked the question.

So before asking, know *exactly* what is the information or explanation that you are seeking first. Bear in mind, too, that often when we ask questions we may be relying on certain assumptions and presuppositions. However the listener may not share the same assumptions, presuppositions as we do. Hence the listener may have a different **interpretation** of the question, or he might not understand you at all. For example, have you ever had a conversation with someone who uses a lot of technical jargon that is peculiar only to his trade? Unless you're also in the same trade, most of the jargon wouldn't make sense. This makes the conversation unintelligible. So make it clear to the listener what you want to know.

If necessary, break your questions into smaller parts. Phrase the question as clearly as possible. One-line questions frequently work best as it eliminates variables that may yield differing answer given different situations. Group the questions into categories so that the listener knows that you are discussing about a specific topic, and not jumping from one topic to another.

Don't be afraid to ask questions that may appear "dumb". Especially regarding information that form the basis of more complicated subject matters. It is crucial to have the foundation correct, so that the assumptions and premises that resting on these foundations are correct.

Better to know truth rather than to assume to know it. The damage from ignorance may be worse than a bruised ego.

Finding a role model

A common exhortation to beginners is that they should find someone who has already succeeded in that chosen activity and make that person a role model. Whilst the role model method is a good technique, we should not apply it wholesale without putting any thought into what we are doing.

Before we look for a role model to emulate, we must consider two important factors. Firstly our purpose, i.e. why are we choosing that particular person as a role model, and secondly, our focus, i.e. which aspect of the role model's life or area of expertise are we seeking to emulate? Understanding these two factors is establishing the "big picture", the end state that we wish to attain. Here are some points that need consideration:

1. what do we want to say to ourself and to the world by our choice of a role model?
2. who are the role models who most closely reflect the ideals, values, and the message that we want to convey?
3. what are the attitudes, values and beliefs that these models have in order to create the standards and quality of work? These must align with our personal values to be effective. But even if they don't fully align with ours, all is not lost, as they can be adapted to more effectively suit our needs.
4. Come from a position of <u>understanding</u> when copying processes and practices, not blind rote learning.

Understanding allows more effective application of the processes and practices. Secondly, it allows for modification to suit our own unique needs and disposition. Progress can only come with understanding. I will touch on the topic of understanding in greater detail in the next chapter.

5. Frequently we assume that as long as we slavishly copy what our role model is doing, the pieces will fall into place and success will follow. We may also assume that by following blindly, we will in time come to understand. That is a big assumption because unless we actively strive to understand what we are doing, we frequently are content with just copying blindly.

6. Whatever we are emulating must be with the intention and purpose of improving who *we* are. That remains the primary objective of this venture. Copy the role model's beliefs, attitudes and values, but apply them in <u>your</u> life.

7. The idea is <u>not</u> to become a clone. Emulating your role model is to bring out the best of who you are, and not become a clone of your role model! A clone is just a shadow of the original. And who wants that? In any case, it's impossible to completely copy our models to the smallest details. We are different physically, mentally and emotionally.

8. Fine-tuning - this is the icing on the cake. You can do the same thing, or create your own. After all, you're not a clone. Do what's unique to you. It's also a motivational factor, as it encourages you to define yourself.

Planning - how much is needed?

We often become paralysed over how much planning we must do before embarking on a new venture. Behind this worry is a desire to get things right the very first time. In other words, we don't want to fail. One possible way is to set aside a fixed period of time to find out as much information as you can about the various issues, make the necessary planning. But once the deadline comes up, you must take action. Don't allow yourself just one more day, week or month to think about it. This just makes you lazy and procrastinate.

However undertaking new endeavours is never an exact science. We will inevitably learn as we go along. It's only by taking action, making mistakes and learning that we develop the ability to be better prepared for new endeavours in the future. So we can only increase our reservoir of experience by constantly taking action, practicing in order to sharpen our skills in making better and more accurate assessments of what needs to be done in future endeavours.

Starting off gradually.

It's been said elsewhere, but it's worth reiterating: when embarking on a change in lifestyle or a new habit, start gradually. That's the secret. What is "gradual" will vary from one person to another. However it should be a change that is noticeable. You are the best judge of what you are able to commit to.

> The man who moves a mountain begins by moving small stones.

Introducing too many changes at once is a very jarring experience. Firstly, creating changes means disrupting existing life routines. It takes tremendous effort to be able to remember many new variations occurring at once. Therefore there is a high possibility that you may overlook a new routine.

Secondly, it requires willpower to make a change permanent. And willpower is an exhaustible resource. If you implement too many changes at once, this means your willpower will be depleted at a much faster rate; having to pay attention to implementing the changes and resisting temptations to revert to old habits. Once your reserve of willpower is depleted, you will lapse into your old habits and routines.

Thirdly, implementing any change inevitable affects the lives and the routines of the people around you. Introducing too many changes at once make it difficult for them to accommodate these changes on short notice. The more disruptions these changes cause to, the less supportive (if not hostile) the people around will become towards your efforts, thereby reducing your chances of success.

These are just some reasons why many overly-ambitious plans fail. No point being overambitious and starting off at the extreme end, but with no hope of sustaining it in the long term. So always introduce changes slowly and incrementally.

The Art of the Start

Starting anew requires a considerable amount of mental and physical effort. Don't underestimate how much will be needed of you, otherwise you will give up. You have to become accustomed both physically and mentally to new procedures, activities and changes to your existing lifestyle. So be prepared to invest a much greater amount of time and effort at the beginning of any new venture. Later on once the mind and body has acquired the necessary competency, the amount of effort and energy needed to keep going will seem less. How long will the process take? It will vary from one person to another. However the amount of determination and commitment you invest will play a significant role.

Let's use weight-loss as an example again. If you've decided to go on a diet, starting gradually may mean not taking your favourite food off your grocery list altogether. You could start off by reducing the quantity or the frequency you consume it. For instance, you may skip one fast food meal in a week. Over time, you could reduce the frequency of the fast food meals together with the adoption of healthier food choices. Over time, you might realise that you don't have any craving for fast food anymore.

Coupling the diet program with an exercise regime (which you start gradually) will increase the rate at which you will lose body weight. Start exercising at a frequency and intensity that you are comfortable with. Run a kilometer a day and you will do seven kilometers a week. It beats running all seven kilometers in one single day.

Once you find that you've settled into this new lifestyle of diet and exercise, this is now your new comfort zone. Stretch yourself by increasing the frequency and intensity of your exercise program. For instance, if you can run a kilometer without breaking a sweat, increase the distance to one and a half kilometers. Then two. Then three. With persistence, you will see that the distance you can cover in a week would have increased from seven kilometers to twenty-one! You can also change the type of exercises that you do, for instance, from running to swimming, or perhaps weight training[4]. The idea is not to allow yourself to remain stagnant for too long and to constantly push the confines of your comfort zone ever larger. Over time the incremental efforts will accumulate and you will notice the dramatic changes in your overall well-being and physique.

Once you have achieved your desired body weight, you may find that you are no longer as keen to continue with the diet and exercise program. This is because the original reasons that made you decide to lose weight may have been satisfied. Therefore in order to keep at it, you will need to find new reasons that resonate with the new you. The idea is to make the change into a new habit, so that it becomes an integral part of your life.

This technique can be applied to a whole host of other activities or goals that are related to your studies, work, or general

---

[4]   The shelves of your local bookstore are stocked with books on health, fitness and exercise. Each book proffers its own unique programme. No one book will have the one-size-fits-all solution. Pick one that resonates with you and your lifestyle and which you feel you can stick to in the long run.

self-improvement. The trick is to start of gradually. Remember that for lifestyle changes and introducing new habits, it may take time to get the ingredients of success together. Just as a farmer slowly brings a sapling to a fully grown plant, we too must nourish, protect and care for the new ideas, attitudes and habits that we wish to adopt. Just as a plant does not grow to maturity overnight, our new ideas, attitudes and habits require a period of time to take root and establish itself.

Sticking to the diet

Often times you may abandon a diet program because of stress and you are looking for a way to relieve it. Or if you go through a bad patch in a relationship, and food is a form of solace. Or after long tiring day, you just don't seem to have the willpower to resist that tub of ice cream.

But if you think about it, what has **that** life situation got to do with your diet? Why are you directing the stress at work at the food that's going into your body? Resist the urge to go off track whenever you encounter an obstacle in an unrelated area. As soon as you become aware of that familiar urge to grab a bite, stop yourself from falling back into that old habit.

Difficult as it may sound, find an alternative outlet or release that is positive, rather than one that sets you back on another aspect of your life. Take charge of yourself, and overcome that momentary urge to put something in your mouth. Listen to music. Talk to someone. Or take a walk. Once that momentary urge passes, you will have stayed on course with your diet just that much longer.

Instant gratification

We live in a world where we expect instant results. We find answers on the Internet in a fraction of a second. Goods we order arrive in mere days, when they used to take weeks. Communications via e-mail and video mean that we are constantly in touch. Such is the pace of our lifestyle that we also expect personal development to take place at this velocity.

However the best things in life require an investment of time and effort. You will also come to realise that the joys in life are often discovered and experienced during the process of working towards the results. And quite often there's more joy in the journey than in the destination itself. Whilst the lure and seduction of instant results will always call to us, we should not be tempted, and be steadfast disciples of effort, discipline and commitment.

We don't go straight from sowing to harvesting. Cultivation, namely the process of working persistently towards the desired results are still necessary. There no shortcuts.

Setting loftier goals

Over time you will become familiar with the process of setting goals and achieving them. It is then time to be a bit more ambitious and set goals that will stretch you.

I'd like to use an analogy. Let's say we are throwing a pebble that we've picked up as we are walking along a road. At first, we throw the pebble by just a flick of our wrist. We then progress to throwing the pebble using the strength of just our forearm. Further along, we begin throwing the stone with our entire arm employing the strength of our shoulder. Finally you try throwing the stone with all your might. The distance in which the stone travels gets further and further way as we deploy more of our strength. It will take us longer and longer to walk up to where the stone falls before we can pick it up to throw it again. The road represents the path of our life.

The act of throwing the pebble represents the goals that we set along the way. In the same way, we can initially set goals that are easy to attain. However in order to push ourselves and discover what we are truly capable of, we have to set goals that progressively require more effort to achieve.

Now that we've set off on our journey, let's consider the factors that keep us moving along and the obstacles we will encounter along the way.

What keeps us going

Effort

Why is effort important in the context of keeping us going towards our goal? Often once the excitement and novelty of starting a new venture has worn off, we are left with the realisation of the long tiring grind ahead of us. It's the willingness to put in the effort to grind through what needs to be done day after day, week after week, month after month that gets us to the finish line eventually.

There is no sugar-coating this immutable fact of life: Everything worthwhile achieving requires effort. A lot of effort. It is the price that has to be paid to reach each and every one of your desired life goals. Contrary to popular belief, there really are no shortcuts in life. Shortcuts may yield short term results, but a worthwhile goal always requires an investment of both time and effort.

The other reality of life is that real success in life can't be acquired through "hire purchase". By this I mean that you can't enjoy the fruits of the labour before the labour. Give me the university degree now, and I will study later. Give me the trim and fit body now, and I will work out in the gym later. Give me the million dollars now, and I will work for it later.

The willingness to put in the effort to our chosen cause is one of the factors that set those who achieve, apart from those who merely wish and passively dream of what could be. We see this willingness happening globally when men and women, especially from developing countries, who are hungry and determined to succeed will head towards the countries and industries with the greatest opportunities. They are prepared to work harder and longer hours, usually at a lower salary. Although statistically the percentage of these truly determined individuals is very small compared to the total population of that country, however if you happen to be living in that a country or working in that industry, you will need to be be prepared to work even harder to remain "average".

Motivation

Motivation is defined as a reason or reasons for acting in a particular way. Unlike knowledge, motivation cannot be imparted from one person to another. We can only share the circumstances or the factors by which motivation can be instilled. Or we could artificially "create" motivation by either dangling a carrot or wielding a stick. Nevertheless as we have seen earlier, a reason that is introduced externally will not be as compelling a reason that comes from within ourselves.

Similarly true motivation cannot be introduced externally. It is a force that must come from within oneself. Motivation can be broadly placed into two different categories. One category is what can be referred to as a positive motivation (the carrot) whereas the the other category can be referred to as a negative motivation (the stick).

A positive motivation is something that drives us towards a goal or a desired end result. It is usually associated with a pleasant experience or emotion. Examples of a positive motivation or "reward" would be a job promotion, a shopping trip, or a vacation. More complex or intangible motivational factors can be the desire to satisfy the need for self-actualisation.

On the other side of the spectrum, a negative motivation is a discomfort or (usually) a punishment that you want to get away from. A example of this would be a parent threatening to take away a child's privileges if he doesn't complete his school work, or in the case of a working adult, a pay cut or demotion.

Both will compel us to action. Both forms of motivation may also have a strong experiential resonance. But one is an incentive-based whereas the other is a disincentive. It is my view that whenever it is possible, you should associate positive motivational factors to to your desired goal. Here is why. A negative motivator does not compel us to excel or to do better. We will be motivated to take action only until the discomfort or threat of punishment is gone. But we will go no further since there is no incentive to do so.

This creates a mediocre mindset which will have far-reaching ramifications to our life as a whole. We will experience a lifestyle where we are content to merely subsist at a level above any form of discomfort, and no more. A positive motivational force, on the other hand, ensures that we continue to strive until we achieve what we desire. Often in the course of doing so, we push ourselves to do more than what we originally thought we could do. Therefore always a adopt a positive motivational factor over a negative one.

Persistence and Consistency

> Because life's not a 100-meter sprint, but a marathon. And it's a marathon that you have to continue running just to keep what you have, let alone garner more of. The greater the stakes, the greater the effort that's expected.

Every successful life goal is a result of persistent effort. Mere positive thinking and visualisation will not bring you any tangible results unless you persist with your physical efforts until the results manifest. It's the act of taking, and *continuing* to take, one small step at a time, pushing the project onwards even when it seems there is little, if any, results to show for your efforts.

Successful achievement of any goal is a product of consistent effort, as opposed to sporadic or one-off action. Getting to the goal is dependent on the small routine things we do every day. It may be simple acts like waking up early, taking time to practise, keeping to routines punctually and being disciplined about it. We choose to take action even when we are tired, or are simply feeling lazy and don't really feel up to it. These are little things that seem insignificant when considered in isolation. However their effect as a whole will be what separates the excellent from the merely average. Persistence and consistency makes all the difference in the world.

Everyone loves simple answers. Solutions that are easy to understand, and even easier to implement. If it's something that you need to do just once, all the better! Alas, there are no shortcuts. The bigger the goals that you set, the longer the road that you may have to travel to achieve success. And it's a road that you will often travel alone. At times the road may seem unbearably difficult and you don't see how you could ever pull it off. That's when having reasons with great experiential resonance will help you stay the course during these difficult periods of time. Remind yourself that the goal is already achieved, and that you are simply moving towards it. Staying on the road can be lonely, painful and tiring. But that's why not everyone who starts out will eventually reach their goals. That is also why the rewards waiting at the end are reserved for the truly deserving.

> Don't stop where you run out of steam. Or where inspiration runs out. You stop at your goal's end. To stop anywhere else is to acknowledge that the goal as unattainable. To acknowledge that defeat and failure has claimed you. It's perfectly alright to stop, rest and recover your strength. But remember to get up once again, cast off all thoughts of defeat and plough on.

Harnessing the power of habits

Habits are routine processes we adopt to help us perform repetitious tasks more efficiently without the need to commit too much mental resources. Habits ensure we minimise mistakes. What is interesting is that no matter how complex the task may be, with sufficient repetition we develop processes that enable us to run these complex tasks on autopilot, as it were. We are therefore able to handle complex albeit mundane tasks whilst channeling our attention to other tasks at the same time, for instance, we are able to drive to work whilst talking on the phone at the same time.

Our habits play a significant role in our lives, both at a macro level as well as on the micro level. Whether we are are aware of it, our habits determine how we do our work, what we do in our free time, how we react to people, and the decisions we make regarding our lives. Remember however that habits have to serve you, to improve your quality of life, and not prevent you from achieving your goals. There are bad habits that we adopt, consciously or otherwise. Like having to munch on something when you're watching TV. Checking your email compulsively, even when you're not expecting anything important to come in.

Secondly, we should not allow our lives to run as if it were an automated routine of processes, just like a computer program, from the day's beginning to its end. Otherwise it's no different than sleepwalking through life. You may be conscious of what is taking place, but feel helpless and unable to stop it.

You need to be aware of the relevance of these habits. Analyse your daily routines, and be conscious of whether there are habits in place that you <u>aren't</u> even aware of. Routines may be taking place in very small things, such as how you place your cup, or arrange your books on the shelf, to more significant issues, such as your budgeting, spending habits, how you talk to your loved ones, etc. Discard that which do not serve you, and adopt new habits that do.

In his excellent book, *"The Power of Habit"* by Charles Duhigg, he described habits as consisting of three main components, namely a cue (the trigger), the routine (which occurs when a person perceives the cue) and the reward (the satisfying of a craving that manifests itself when the cue appears). I would strongly encourage you to read the book to have a better understanding of our habits, and how we can change them.

For instance, the book explains why we lapse into a routine whenever we encounter the cue, even though we have no desire for the reward. You may identify with this situation if you wonder how the packet of potato chips just appears in your hands, as if by magic, whenever you sit down in front of the TV! Charles Duhigg also explores the possibility that the reward we crave from the habit may not necessarily be satisfied by the process itself. For instance, a smoker may not smoke to satisfy the craving for nicotine, but may be doing it to relieve boredom. The same could be same of a person who habitually checks his mobile phone for incoming emails. It may not be because he wishes to remain in contact, but it may be to distract himself during moments of inactivity or avoid having to make conversation in a social situation.

This is not to suggest that the eradication of a bad habit or the institution of a new habit will be easy but it is good to understand the mechanics of something that we take for granted, so that the our efforts in making changes are more effective and efficient.

> Remember that you decide the habits to form. You have the power to change them. Habits are there to serve you. Don't allow them to control you.

Harnessing our existing mindset and physiology of success

Whenever you are taking on a new activity or skill that is challenging, here's a technique that you can try. Think of a challenging task that you perform regularly, and which you excel in. Even though this task may take a considerable amount of effort (whether physically or mentally) to complete, you are always certain that you are able to complete it successfully. This task may take different forms, for instance a 10km run, preparing the department's monthly performance report, or giving a sales presentation to a potential customer.

Now imagine the state of mind, the feelings and physiology that you have whenever you are carrying out this task. The idea is to recreate the habitual good experience (engaging as many of our five senses, as well as our mental and emotional state) that we have come to associate with this particular activity and "superimpose" this mindset, physiology and emotional state onto this new activity when you are performing it. Go about the new activity in the same way that you would in the activity that you have chosen for this technique. Move and act with a sense of purpose and certainty, confident in your abilities.

The objective of this technique is not to create a belief premised on the fact that since we have succeeded in the first activity, we will therefore succeed in the new one, too. Such a belief may not always produce the desired results, since there is no previous experience with this new activity that we can create a mental construct on. Rather our intention is to harness the mindset and physiology of successful achievement through effort. What the mind is programmed to "see", it is programmed to deliver. We recreate an attitude that we will prevail over this new activity even if it may prove a challenge.

Over time you will realise that the mindset and physiology of excellence has always been inherent, and can be "activated" at will. It is then possible to skip the process of finding an activity that you excel in, because you now realise that you can excel in whatever that you do.

Handling stress from multiple demands

Here's a "walkthrough" on coping with those life situations when problems are coming at us in thick and fast, and the pressure just seems too great. This may occur at work (which is often the case) but this can happen in other areas of life, too. However whatever the situation, I hope these pointers will help you keep a level head, and perhaps thrive in such situations!

Physiology

- Remember to breathe! We frequently hold our breath unconsciously when we are overwhelmed. Or we breathe in short sharp gasps. Take in your breaths slowly and deliberately. When you do this, you unconsciously calm both your mind and body. In this way, you ensure that you maintain a greater sense of situational awareness.
- Consciously relax the body. Be aware if your body is feeling tense, in particular, the muscles in the region of the shoulders and neck as they cause you to feel tired.
- Stay calm mentally. Be aware of the emotions that you are feeling. Are you feeling panic, fear or restlessness? Maintain focus and move your mind away from negative emotions and thoughts. Shed all unnecessary mental chatter. Ignore any thoughts that are unnecessary or irrelevant to completing the tasks before you now.
- Consciously "slow" down the passage of time in the mind. In the face of mounting pressure and demands, our mind unconsciously starts to race. This in turn causes our heart to start racing as well. So mentally "slow" down the passage of time. Our mind is conditioned to go "forward", to be somewhere else other than here and now. Be acutely aware of the **present** moment. Tell yourself that there is no where to go to. And you only need to address the issue before you **right now.**

- Consciously make the effort to slow down your train of thoughts. Making decisions in a hurried state of mind rarely yields good outcome. Contrary to what it seems, making slow and deliberate decisions make for more efficient and effective work flow. Haste (whether mental or physical) often increase the likelihood of mistakes. It is better to ensure that the task is done once, and done correctly.

- Focus your attention as if it were a beam of light from a torchlight in a dark room. You will direct your "beam" of attention at the immediate task at hand, and no where else, so that the rest of the other tasks are in the "dark" for the moment. Don't flit your attention about amongst the tasks. It's like flicking a torchlight all over the place in a dark room. It will just get you disorientated. As you improve, you will learn to reduce the "area" of the light so as to eliminate distraction. Be very conscious of all your movements. In fact, be as deliberate as possible with all your actions and movements. Shed off all unnecessary motions and actions.

Practical considerations

- Organise the tasks into similar categories and, within the categories themselves, according to the level of urgency. Of course, if there are matters of very pressing urgency, these should be dealt with first, regardless of which category they fall into.

- Have a notebook or a notepad nearby, so that incoming emails, phone calls and tasks can be written down and not forgotten in the midst of the chaos. These additional tasks can be attended to once the more pressing ones are dealt with.

- Focus on each item of work at hand. At times of extreme stress, the mind often wanders and speculate on worst case scenarios. This is an unfruitful, and a waste of time and energy. Whenever you notice your mind wandering, bring it back to the task at hand. Develop a laser-like focus and an ability to tune out the surrounding and extraneous noise.

- If work needs to be delegated, do so calmly and with the necessary details so that it can carried with as little supervision as possible. It will not help your cause if the information is incomplete, and your colleagues, friends or family members keep coming back for more clarifications.
- Once the situation has resolved itself, give yourself a pat on the back. You would have done great being able to withstand the pressures the circumstances imposed on you. But also take to assess how you may have handled the situation(s) better. Learn from them and improve your performance in the future.

Confronting adversity

- You must have absolute certainty that will reach the goal eventually. No matter how long it may take. You should not doubt that you will eventually reach the destination.
- Look at the situation as if the end result is already manifested, and that it's just a process of working towards the *completed* result.
- Notwithstanding what others may suggest, so long as you are in the driver's seat, you *have* to make the decisions on how to proceed based on *your* own instincts.
- Even if you don't see all the signs along the road, trust your instincts to guide you along the right path. Trust your abilities.
- You have to persevere even if the people on board aren't able to render any assistance. You must have the courage, determination and a clear mind to persist.

> - Anticipate the obstacles ahead, rather than reacting to them.
> - Never give up. Don't get angry when things don't go your way. Don't blame others or be upset with them. Remain calm in spite of adversity.
> - This is when we walk our talk. Remember that each adversity is a lesson, and an opportunity to put our beliefs into practice.
> - Give thanks to God when you succeed.

Obstacles that we encounter along the way

"Problem: An unwelcome or harmful matter needing to be dealt with and overcome, a thing that is difficult to achieve" - Oxford English Dictionary

The four categories of problems

In the course of life, we inevitably encounter numerous obstacles, crises, and problems. Some of these problems will occur time and again in recognisable patterns. At one time or another, they make us want to throw in the towel. These patterns can be categorised into four main categories that I will refer to as the wall, the plateau, the pile-up, and the vicious cycle.

The Wall

The wall is characterised by a singular problem that appears insurmountable at first glance. It just doesn't seem like there is a way to even begin to come to grips with the issue. It may be a huge logistical or physical challenge. For instance, it may be implementing a new policy in the office that is unpopular with the entire rank and file of the department. Or starting an exercise and dieting program from scratch. Or starting a new business. Or moving to a new house.

The sheer and magnitude of the challenge overwhelms our mind and we feel helpless and unprepared to take it on. We lack the confidence and courage to start. The temptation is to not even begin at all as the obstacle just seems so insurmountable.

The Plateau

If the Wall is the 400-pound gorilla standing in your path, the plateau is like a long flat road running through a big dry featureless desert, with no end in sight. We might seem to remain where we are despite our persistence and best efforts. And the worst thing is we can't put our finger on the cause of our stagnation. We encounter the plateau in the office when we hit a glass ceiling that prevents us from further advancement. We are labouring through our exercise and dieting program, but aren't seeing any further improvement. We experience a sense of hopelessness, disappointment and frustration. We might even feel that we are destined never to reach our goal. So why waste more time and energy trying? We become tempted to quit the endeavour and try something new.

The Pile-Up

The pile-up is not a single obstacle, but is comprised of a multitude of problems that surface simultaneously and each of them demanding your immediate attention. Whenever you encounter a pile-up, it's like fighting a multi-headed hydra. We take a lot of time, energy and resources dealing with one crisis after another. And at the end of it, we are no closer to our primary goal. The problems in the pile-up may be related to the goal we are working on, or they may concern other areas of our lives, unrelated to the goal itself. Nevertheless we are forced to divert our attention, energy and resources to resolve them.

Just like the wall, a pile-up can create in us a sense of being thoroughly overwhelmed by life situations. However in this case, the magnitude of the problems may be smaller, just significantly greater in number. If you're running your own business, for example, pile-ups may come in the form of staff resignations, manpower shortages, equipment breaking down, complaints from customers, issues with existing work. Each of the problems, if not addressed immediately will likely adversely affect the company's performance and reputation. Whilst on the home front, your children's grades are deteriorating, the car needs to be serviced, the laundry's piling up, and to compound matters, you're fighting a flu.

Thoughts like 'Why me?' or 'It's not fair' can crop up, especially if the life situations are unforeseen and not of our doing. The problems just seem to be beating us into submission. Pile-ups also cause a sense of frustration as we are prevented from allocating our time and precious resources to doing what we really want.

The Vicious Cycle

The vicious cycle can appear in the form of a single problem, but it usually manifests as a cluster of problems (e.g. a pile-up). It is possible to encounter cyclical plateaus, too. What is unique about the vicious cycle is that the problems keep recurring. They may even appear in specific intervals like clockwork on a weekly, monthly or even annual basis.

Vicious cycles are a classic example of where we merely address the immediate issues without asking why we are constantly facing these issues over and over again. You might experience situations where you survive a pile-up, have a slight breather before another pile-up hits you. The cycle may occur on a weekly, monthly or even yearly basis. As we are constantly in a state of fire-fighting, often with the same problems, we exist in a state of survival mode. We rarely, if ever, have the chance to even look at the big picture. The vicious cycle leaves us feeling thoroughly exhausted both physically and mentally. We might also get the feeling that we have bitten off more than we can chew, since the problems keep coming at us in never-ending waves.

Here's a classic example of a vicious cycle. You put off your Christmas shopping until the last weekend before Christmas. You panic when you realise you don't have much time left, and rush about drawing up your Christmas gifts list. You rush out to the mall and end up being stuck in traffic jams. Once you arrive at your destination, you spend more time looking for a place to park the car. You fight your way through the shopping malls that are packed with last-minute shoppers and have to endure long lines at the checkout counters. By the time Christmas actually arrives, you're exhausted, worn-out and cranky from all that rushing. You vow to either start shopping earlier when Christmas comes around next year. But the ritual repeats itself again when *next* Christmas comes around!

Finding a solution

Each category of problem listed above impedes our progress in their own unique way. While they may share some common features, each obstacle requires its own unique solution. And to do so, I recommend adopting a structured approach to problem-solving. Having a structured, logical approach enables us to (i) identify what solutions will works for us, and what doesn't, (ii) troubleshoot the process, (iii) identify the solution, and the steps that we can replicate should the problem arise again.

And problems usually do re-appear, albeit in a different form or in another aspect of our lives. It would be a waste of our time and energy to have overcome a problem once, forget how we solved it and spend more time and resources finding out how to do it again.

Here are the suggested steps:

- identifying the immediate problems;
- identifying the root problems. This is a crucial step, as most of the time, we will stop as soon as we identify the immediate problems before us;
- identifying the causes of both categories of problems; and

- identifying the solutions and implementing them.

Identifying the immediate problems as well as their causes is usually easy. At this stage, the temptation is to come up with a solution to solve the immediate problem at hand. Most of the time, we are content to just stop at this stage, and get on with our lives. However as we shall see in the case of vicious cycles, if we are focused only on resolving the immediate problems, this is merely a stop-gap measure, since the problems will repeat themselves again and again.

However it is better to take the effort to peel back the layers of the immediate problems. By carrying out this analysis, we might realise that each of the immediate problems (especially with problems in the form of a plateau, pile-up and vicious cycle) are merely the symptoms of the core problem. And the core problem may be totally unrelated to each of the problems or collectively. For example, the core problem could be poor time management. By managing our time better, the problems may be resolved completely, or at least we are able to prepare for them in advance and ameliorate its effect. We will often find that once we resolve the root cause of the problem, most of the immediate problems will disappear altogether; thereby reducing the number of remedial steps we need to take and making the remaining steps easier to implement.

> "When you first start off trying to solve a problem, the first solutions you come up with are very complex, and most people stop there. But if you keep going, and live with the problem and peel more layers of the onion off, you can often times arrive at some very elegant and simple solutions." - Steve Jobs

The Four Root Causes of Problems

All problems that we encounter, however complex or simple, whether in our personal, social or work lives have their origins from one or a combination of four root causes. I will refer to these four root causes as (i) our comfort zone, (ii) change, (iii) ignorance, and (iv) time management.

What is interesting to note is that all four root causes are **internal** issues. In other words, they are issues that relate to our willingness to transcend what we are comfortable with, our ability to adapt to changes or to create change, the quality of the information we have, as well as the way we make use of our information and experience. Lastly it relates to the way we use our time. The external problems that are occurring in our lives are simply a **consequence** of these internal issues. This is good news, as it means that once we resolve these internal issues, the problems we encounter in our life will be resolved as well! The ultimate solutions to our problems are all **within** our control. However to be able to "see" the root causes of the problems we encounter, we need to step out of the picture frame and to look at the picture as a whole, rather than just the details. We shall now explore each category of root causes.

Comfort Zone

Of the four root problems, it is my view that the comfort zone constitutes a major cause of a substantial number of problems that we encounter. The comfort zone can be defined as the level at which we can live and function with a sense of ease and familiarity. It can also be described as an accustomed environment (real or perceived) in which we exist. By remaining in our comfort zone, we avoid hardship, inconvenience and risk of failure since as we are only doing what we are accustomed to. After all, we can't fail if we don't try anything new!

Ironically the comfort zone might be painful. Yet we would rather feel the pain of the known rather than the fear and uncertainty of the unknown. And although the comfort zone is purely a mental construct without any real physical presence, it might as well be one as it feels like a walled-off area beyond which we don't venture beyond. We develop an unhealthy attachment to its confines whether we are conscious of it or not.

Each of us exist in a comfort zone in one form or another. It may be as simple as our hesitation in smiling at the stranger whom we always meet in the elevator on our way to office. Or eating only the same kind of food, prepared in the same way. Here is a way you can test this hypothesis. If you have ever experienced actual physical pain or discomfort, or felt upset, depressed, annoyed, frustrated, violated, disappointed or any other negative emotion when you encounter something different or out of the ordinary, that physical or emotional discomfort tells you that you have reached the boundaries of your comfort zone.

One of the characteristics of the comfort zone is that it creates an aversion to change, whether it is a change that's actually taking place or a change that needs to happen in order for us to get to our goals. We see this happening in the plateau and vicious cycle.

In the case of the plateau, we may lose sight of the reason why we are doing that thing. Very soon the process becomes the end itself, rather than the means to the end. Our drive and enthusiasm suffer since we don't have a strong and compelling reason to make us want to improve. The vicious cycle is an example of where the comfort zone is painful, yet we would rather put up with this pain rather than to overcome the inertia of finding a way out of this unproductive cycle. We know that the status quo is unacceptable, but we find excuses ("I don't have the time" or "I'm too tired") just so we don't have to find a solution.

The comfort zone is the invisible barrier that separates the average from those who experience great levels of success. For very few want to venture beyond the confines of their areas of comfort, no matter how narrow that area may be. For those of us who desire to differentiate ourselves from others, this desire alone will be sufficient incentive to constantly strive to expand the limits of our comfort zone, to the point that we can act spontaneously and without hesitation regardless of what the situation calls for.

To overcome our comfort zone, we must firstly be aware that we are in one. Otherwise we will remain in a state of denial. To transcend its confines, your desire for your goal must surpass the discomfort of getting to it. Discard the illusion that you can be or have something by remaining who you are right now.

The comfort zone is a mental construct. It is simply a creation of our mind, and has no real physical existence. But it is our **belief** that it exists that enables it to have such a strong restrictive influence over our lives. If we can come to terms with, or condition ourselves to not react negatively to adverse conditions or experiences in whatever form they may appear, the walls of our comfort zone will disappear. If we stop comparing our current state with the past or imagined future, and just experience the present as it is, it quite likely that we are able to endure what we previously considered impossible.

Having a lot persistence helps, as we need to overcome the inertia of starting something new, or to resist the pull of our old habits. Create new habitual patterns to (i) consciously overwrite the old habits and (ii) shift the focus away from the discomfort to the benefits that the change will bring about. Lastly, celebrate any improvements that any step out of the comfort zone has brought about, however small it may seem to be. With persistence, we will breach our comfort zone more frequently and take ever bigger steps out of that zone.

> "You must be willing to do the things today that others won't, in order to have the things tomorrow others won't have." - Les Brown.

Change

Paradoxically change is the only one thing that is permanent in life. Things grow old and break down, people leave or die, opinions change, our competitors improve. Even weather patterns change! For the purposes of our discussion, change becomes a root cause of problems because (i) things that used to work, cease working or (ii) things are working fine, but in order for us to achieve our goals, we need to change the way things work.

In the first category, change causes problems when we fail to take it into account as we assume that what works for us will continue to work indefinitely. It's an inevitable fact of life that we will experience change whether we want it or not, or whether we are aware that it is taking place or not. However because we don't take any steps to anticipate or to cater for change when it happens, it disrupts the way of life that we are accustomed.

We see this occurring in our business when a recession hits the economy, or because our customers' habits and preferences change, or when new competitors enter the market. We see it happening in the quality of our health as we age or if don't care for our body. We see it in our relationships with our children as they grow older and become more independent. In these instances, we will need to take change in stride to **maintain** the current status quo.

Change is a problem in the second category when we are unable to make the lifestyle changes in order to attain the goals that we want. For instance, we know that we have to change our eating habits to overcome our obesity, but we are so comfortable with our current lifestyle. We know that we have to set aside money to invest, but we don't do it because it means having less to buy the things we desire. We know we need to study now for the exams that are coming up at the end of the semester, but we would rather spend our time playing our favourite video game.

To deal with change you have to:

- be aware that change is taking place, or is about to take place. Change may have a direct or indirect impact on you. It may take place internally within your organisation or externally. And change may be controllable or uncontrollable;
- understand and anticipate the consequences that change will have on you, your life, your activities, or in your

relationships. With this understanding, you can see the possibilities and opportunities that change opens up for us;

- take action to take advantage of this change to your benefit, in contrast to just maintaining the status quo.

---

5 Rules of Being Human

Rule #1: you will learn lessons.

Rule #2: there are no mistakes - only lessons.

Rule #3: a lesson is repeated until it is learned.

Rule #4: if you don't learn the early lessons, they get *harder*.

(Pain is one way the universe gets your attention)

Rule #5: you'll know you've learnt a lesson when your actions change.

- John C. Maxwell, *Failing Forward*.

Ignorance

In the context of this topic, I am using the word "ignorance" to identify three issues. Firstly, the quality of our information; secondly, the failure to use the wealth of knowledge and experience to develop wisdom; and thirdly, the failure to analyse and reflect.

Quality of information

It's really quite easy to see how ignorance can cause problems to arise. The quality of the decisions we make and the actions we take are dependent on the quality of our information and knowledge. The better the quality of the information, the better our decisions and performance. Conversely if the information or knowledge that we rely on is wrong or unreliable, our decisions and actions would be adversely affected.

The quality of our knowledge or information on any issue can fall into three broad categories: (i) non-existent information.

This encompasses situations where we are aware of our absolute lack of information or where we are unaware that we are ignorant, (ii) incomplete information or (iii) information that is wrong or inaccurate (for instance, if the information is outdated).

It's quite easy to be aware of our lack of knowledge on an issue, because if we analyse an issue thoroughly, we will eventually encounter a wall of "fog", through which we can't "see" beyond. This, then, is the limit of our knowledge and information of that subject matter. At this juncture, we can begin listing down exactly what we don't know and need more information on. The challenge comes when we are unaware of the fact that we are ignorant.

For example, we start up a new business venture in a foreign country. We assume that the rules and regulations are identical to that of our own country of origin. We may be unaware of the licences and regulatory approvals that are necessary to operate the business in that country. As a result of which, we may be exposed to potential fines and criminal liability for contravening the laws of that country.

Similarly information that is completely wrong or inaccurate is frequently not detectable until it's too late. Some possible reasons for inaccurate or incomplete information are as follows:

- Not verifying the reliability of the source of information;
- Not verifying the accuracy of the information;
- Not verifying if our information is out-of-date or may be irrelevant due to change;
- not being aware of alternative interpretations of the information;
- not being aware that the accuracy of the information is subject to certain pre-conditions being satisfied;
- not taking the effort to exhaust all avenues of information whether due to pure omission or lack of experience in sourcing for such information.

Our Past

Use the past as a reservoir of knowledge and experience, and not as a gauge of your ability as your previous performances may be a gross underestimate or overestimate of your current or future abilities.

More importantly, do not let what has happened in the past to hold you back from doing what you are truly capable of. For instance, don't look at your previous failed attempts as an indication that you will likely fail again. Because when you do that, your mind will program itself to fail. And what the mind thinks, it will manifest into reality. It's essential to decouple your experience (which is useful) from the past results (which is just an outcome).

Failure to Develop Personal Wisdom

The Oxford English dictionary defines "knowledge" as facts, information, and skills acquired by a person through experience or education. In other words, it is information that we obtain through learning or in the course of living our lives. "Experience" is defined as **practical** contact with and observation of facts or events. The "wisdom" is a derived from the word "wise" which means having or showing experience, knowledge and **good judgment**.

Wisdom though widely sought cannot be taught through a textbook. Whilst knowledge can be transferred and experience shared, wisdom can only be gained by actively reflecting on the information and experience we have gathered in the course of life; by "stepping back" and looking at the big picture of the life situations we are in and gleaning lessons from them. This requires discernment and reflection. To be able to connect and put two and two together. It is being open to changing events, processes to procure a different outcome. Wisdom allows us to evaluate, amongst others, the costs of a certain action, the benefits and the consequences (both direct and indirect). It is therefore easy to see why we **must** to walk life's journey, for without which, wisdom is not attainable even if we spend a lifetime gathering information.

We have all heard of the Biblical tale of King Solomon who decreed that the baby be cut in half to settle the dispute between two women claiming to be its mother. King Solomon showed wisdom in that act, albeit in a very unorthodox way. King Solomon could have used the very conventional way of ascertaining the truth, namely by calling forth witnesses and questioning them, evaluating the credibility of the two women and the evidence at hand before coming to a decision. Quite likely he may have arrived at the same finding as chopping the baby in two. But the unconventional method came from the use of a mix of knowledge and wisdom. Firstly, King Solomon knew of the unconditional love that the real mother has for the child, and that only the real mother would be prepared for the child to live with a stranger, rather than to let it die by the sword. With the benefit of this knowledge, King Solomon was able to arrive at the decision more efficiently. Therefore wisdom (or one aspect of it) is knowing the available solutions to a problem, and choosing the best solution for that given situation.

It is therefore necessary to develop our personal wisdom so that we are better able to navigate through or around the difficulties that life throws at us. With wisdom, we are able to weigh the available options and choose the best course of action under the circumstances.

Failure to analyse

Having the benefit of the wealth of information we have gathered, we are frequently content to allow our pool of information to remain stagnant. We don't take the effort to perceive patterns or trends. We fail to see the cause and effect of events in the information before us. We may also fail to see the things that we can do to live our lives more efficiently and effectively, or avert problems from occurring altogether.

Therefore:

- Don't accept the information you receive at face value. Challenge the credibility and accuracy of the information before you. Failing to verify the accuracy of our information results in our having incomplete or inaccurate information.
- Analyse and interpret the data and see what can be gleaned from it. Get the views of other people, as we all can interpret the same information differently.
- Make it a habit to go beyond just a superficial level of analysis. Go deeper to see if there are other valuable nuggets of insight that you may uncover. Very often our very best ideas will come only after we have invested time and effort in thinking.
- Run "what if" scenarios to anticipate potential issues or to discover possible opportunities.
- Consider how the results of your analysis and reflection can be used to make your life better.

Time Management

Although the problems relating to time management are, ultimately, result from a combination of the other root causes of problems (usually comfort zone and ignorance), however the excuse that "I'm too busy" or "I don't have the time" is cited so frequently, that it deserves to be categorised as a primary cause in itself.

We frequently overlook the role that time management plays in the process of achieving our goals, especially when we begin taking on multiple projects simultaneously, or when we set more complex goals. Remember that when we set bigger goals, our daily life routines and smaller goals still need our attention, too. "I don't have the time" is the very first line of excuse that's often cited, and in fact the one excuse that stops 95% of all attempts at self-improvement dead in their tracks.

I have found that one of the causes for many problems we encounter in the plateau, pile-up and vicious cycle are due to improper time management Time management issues fall into two main categories: inefficient allocation (using too much time) or insufficient allocation (setting aside too little time or outright procrastination).

Inefficient allocation

Time management is ultimately a resource allocation exercise. Excel in it and it reaps great dividends. Fail at it, and it causes a domino effect that affects that particular area of our life, its related tasks; and fanning out to every other part of our lives which may, at first glance, have no connection whatsoever to the initial issue. For instance, a failure to properly prioritise tasks at work may cause other tasks to miss their deadlines. In order to overcome this group of issues, we may have to sacrifice time that we may otherwise spend with our families, or to exercise or for social activities. These compromises may have far reaching consequences in the future that we may not be able to discern at this point in time.

The quality of our work is likely to suffer too since we will be fighting fire on all fronts. This itself creates other consequential problems that will then require our attention in the future. The intangible price we pay far exceeds the ostensible cost of investing the time to address the initial life situation.

> Ironically the sooner we take our eyes off the "time" we need to accomplish something, and focus on the things that need doing, the sooner they are accomplished.

We frequently overestimate our abilities, and underestimate the amount of time each task may take. Although time alone does not bring success, but time is needed to bring the elements necessary for success together. Juggling how we best use the time we have to get the elements into place is crucial. Because we don't priorities our tasks properly and don't carry out our work efficiently, problems begin to crop up. As the old saying goes, "a stitch in time saves nine".

Prioritisation

What is urgent may not be important. Learn to differentiate between the two. Failing to address important important issues dooms us to repeating the same mistakes and facing the same problems over and over again. This is not to suggest that urgent matters do not need to be attended to, but that important ones **must** be addressed and not be kept on the back burner indefinitely. Prioritization also means taking action at the right time. Delaying may compound issues.

Many books have been written on the the subject of time management. One of my personal favourites, and which I highly recommend, is "*Eat the Frog*" by Brian Tracy.

Finding a solution

Now that we gotten to know the four root causes of problems a little better, let's consider how we can address them in the context of the wall, the plateau, the pile-up and the vicious cycle. We have a natural tendency not dwell to on our failures, mistakes and problems in order to improve ourselves. If at all, we rely on them only as excuses to justify our shortcomings. We view problems as one of those unpleasant things that "just happen", and we don't place much importance on them. We just try to overcome them as soon as possible or, if it's possible, push its resolution into the future and get on with life.

However we can adopt an alternative constructive perspective to problems. We can view problems we encounter as opportunities for self-reflection and improvement. We can discern areas where we can improve our inner qualities (mental, physical, emotional), how we do things, how we react to life situations and to the people and the world around us.

It would be truly a tragedy if we never learn from our problems and be doomed to expending time, energy and resources to addressing them over and over again in the future.

The Wall

At first glance, the wall appears to be one huge indomitable problem. On closer examination however, this category of problems can usually be broken down into smaller components. To overcome it, the approach to take is to break the wall into smaller manageable chunks. And once we are able to progressively resolve these smaller chunks, the wall won't seem so indomitable after all! Therefore the first thing to do is to identify the smaller "chunks" or components of the wall so that we are able to address them individually. Be as specific as possible when identifying the smaller issues. Also be as comprehensive as possible, so that all which is giving you cause for concern are written down. Once all these components have been identified, try grouping them into categories, if possible.

Write down the proposed solutions, as well as the steps to getting these solutions. Create a checklist that you can go through on a step-by-step basis. Make your checklist as clear and comprehensive as possible so that you don't leave anything out and are taken by surprise later.

Having created the checklist, determine the ingredients needed for each solution. It may be physical objects such as equipment, resources such as information, or intangibles, such as the advice or assistance from other people. Creating a checklist is an empowering step because in doing so, the wall ceases to be a big intangible obstacle that exists only in your mind. It has taken form and you can come to grips with it. The wall has become simply a list of issues that of more manageable size.

One reason why walls are so daunting is because they are usually problems that we have never encountered before, and therefore have no prior experience or knowledge to fall back on. Walls therefore originate from our lack of information and experience. To overcome this root cause, one of our very first tasks will be to acquire as much information as we can regarding the various issues in order that we consider the options available to us in dealing with them.

Create a list of the action that need to be taken. Where possible, group the tasks into different categories so that they can be performed together. List out the people whom we will require their assistance, things and information that we will need to get the project moving along. Set down the deadlines by which each task needs to be completed. Tick off the completed tasks from the checklist as you progress. If new issues or solutions appear along the way, put them down in the list as well.

You may also want to consider if the problem only "appears" insurmountable because its solutions lie outside the confines of our comfort zone. Consequently in order to resolve the problem, we will have to stretch ourselves beyond what we are accustomed to. Be objective about what needs to be done and gather the necessary determination to do what is needed to overcome the problem.

The Plateau

With plateaus, you need to take to take a different tack since the immediate problems are not readily apparent. You approach this category of problems by highlighting what are the areas that you aren't achieving the desired results. This will be your starting point. You can create broad categories first, and then zero in on the specific areas that need improvement within each broad category. From each specific area you "fan out" to the related activities and requirements, such as the equipment, routines, processes, funding, etc., to see if any of these activities and requirements require tweaking, or an outright change.

However with regard to the root causes, a plateau is predominantly a comfort zone and change-based problems, although ignorance may at times play a role, too.

Why might the plateau be a comfort zone problem? We may have progressed quite far in our journey towards the goal and we have become attached to what we have been doing, and how we have been doing things. We become used to the prevailing status quo. We may be ignorant of this fact, or if we are aware of it, we don't feel that there is any incentive to stretch ourselves. But in order to actually attain the goal itself, we have to go beyond the realm of what we are comfortable with.

We must analyse if there has been a change in how we feel about the reasons upon which we had embarked on this venture in the first place. The experiential resonance that these reasons had in the beginning may not be as strong anymore. Find out why this has happened, and whether it is possible for us to re-connect with these reasons again. Otherwise we can find alternative reasons that resonate with us instead. From the foregoing, you can see that change plays a factor, both as an element that causes what used to work to stop working or it is something that we need to adopt in order to reach our goal.

Change occur in our routines, within ourselves and even the people around us. For instance, in the workplace our team members may no longer share the same level of enthusiasm and passion that we have regarding to our common goal. This could be because they have been entrusted with other projects that are placing demands on their time and resources. Or they could be encountering issues in other areas of their lives. Whatever the reasons may be, we have to analyse the situation and find ways to revitalise our colleagues, or find alternative solutions to pick up the pace where performance is lagging.

If you are encountering a plateau in your weight loss program, it might be that your body has acclimatised itself to your current exercise routines and diet. Making changes to your exercise routines, whether by adopting new exercises or increasing the intensity of your workouts, may help you overcome that sticking point. Tweaking your diet may help, too.

Pile-Up

Since a pile-up consists of many different unrelated problems, the first thing you should do is to list out all the different problems onto a piece of paper. This is so that you have a clear picture of all the problems you need to attend to. Be as specific and comprehensive as possible. Once they are all on paper, see if it's possible to group the problems into categories, so that you may be able to attend to them simultaneously, thereby saving valuable time and resources. Within these categories, you can also list the problems in the order of priority that they need to be resolved.

Then step out of the picture frame, and look at the at the situation you are in as a whole. Do you detect any discernible patterns or trends? Did the problems arise only in the workplace? If so, was it only in respect of certain tasks and involved certain colleagues? Is there any connection between the elements? If it was at home, was it in relation to only certain members of the family, and issues? Have these situations arisen time and again?

At its core, a pile-up is usually caused by a combination of the other root causes. It is a comfort zone issue as it tests our ability to overcome stress imposed by multiple simultaneous demand on our time, attention and resources. Pile-ups also test our ability to maintain focus on what we are doing, as well as to remain emotionally stable in spite of all the demands on us and the ensuing mental chaos they create.

Pile-ups invite us to stretch the limits of our comfort zone, with each encounter we build up an ever larger reservoir of willpower and tolerance. Remind yourself that the problems are merely temporary in nature and will all be resolved eventually.

Problems in this category is also a call to us to analyse why they are occurring in the first place. Could we analyse the immediate problems that we had written down and discern trends and patterns? Discernible patterns allow us to anticipate the problem and cater for them. Are the problems merely symptoms of a deeper core issue? If it is, then addressing the core issue ensures that problems do not recur again.

Is it possible that we were aware that these problems were brewing, but we decided to leave them on the back-burner as they weren't urgent and could be looked at another day? Were there changes taking place in the background that we unaware of (or had allowed by our inaction to take place) which positioned the life situations into a perfect storm? If so, changing our mindset from one that is purely reactionary to a mindset that is anticipatory may prevent the problems from arising in the first place. Alternatively if the problems are unavoidable, by anticipating them, we may be able to prevent them from happening all at the same time.

The vicious cycle

Because vicious cycles usually consist of pile-ups that occur repeatedly, the same steps you take to address the immediate problems in a pile-up can be used here as well. However once you have addressed all the immediate problems and whilst the events are still fresh in your mind, this would be the best time to sit down with a pen and paper and take stock of what had happened.

Try to discern if there are recognisable patterns of events **before** the problems occur, whether the people involved in the issues are the same, or the problems had arisen because of certain actions that we had taken, or failed to do. Note down details of the problems, when it took place, who were involved, and what steps were taken to resolve the problems on this occasion. Make it a habit to practice this process each time you encounter a vicious cycle. With persistent effort, you may be able to discern a commonality amongst the vicious cycles you encounter.

Whilst the vicious cycle is caused by a combination of the other root causes, the fact that a problem is recurring is emblematic of the presence of a comfort zone, as well as an inability or unwillingness to implement changes to break the pattern. We may allow things to be as they are as we are used to our current way of life, notwithstanding the vicious cycles may be source of many sleepless nights, stress and frustration. We choose to accept these unfortunate consequences rather than to explore the possibility of a better alternative.

To paraphrase the familiar saying, insanity is allowing the same things to happen over and over again, and expecting a different result. If you encounter vicious cycles very frequently in the course of your life, it is likely because you have not asserted any control over life's direction. Hence life takes you through a maelstrom of crises over and over again. I proffer a better alternative. Seize control of your life and address these problems.

In the example of the last-minute Christmas shopping, the immediate problems would be finalising the shopping list, determining which shopping malls to visit, finding a car park, etc,. However if we consider the root problems, we will see that why these problems persistently occur every year is because of our comfort zone and perhaps our inability to manage our time properly. We may have become so accustomed to only doing last minute shopping that we are unable to consider the possibility of starting our shopping in November, for instance. Or we whilst we may see the benefits of shopping earlier, however we tend to procrastinate. Thus in order to break this pattern once and for all, we need to take the conscious decision to change our annual Christmas shopping ritual.

I hope that by analysing all problems in the context of the comfort zone, ignorance, change and time management, you will be able to deconstruct the problems to expose the **true** cause(s) of these problems. With sufficient practice, it would become second nature to you to be able to zoom out beyond the immediate problems and spot the real issues. Once you have identified the root causes, you may then take the necessary steps to constructively resolve the core issues, especially the problems that persistently return to bother you time and again.

Other considerations

Deciding when to persevere on, and when to change

For some situations, the decision will come easily. You choose to either persevere with your efforts or change course altogether. For instance, will persistently running longer and longer distances improve your ability to complete a marathon? Yes. However most life situations lie somewhere in spectrum between persistence and change. For instance, if you are encountering a plateau in your weight-loss program, should you persist with it, or would it be beneficial to adopt another program for better results?

What are the factors that may help you determine how to move forward? Firstly, if all factors and circumstances are the same, has your dogged persistence resulted in an advancement towards your desired goal? If you are making progress, albeit slowly, this is a situation where persistence will pay off. If not, a change of tack may be necessary. Let's say that your current lifestyle, attitude and beliefs have not brought you any closer to you life goals. If you are truly committed to attaining your goals, the sensible thing to do would be to change the way you think, your beliefs, your attitude and how you live your life.

Secondly, persistence **can** be change. They are not mutually exclusive. Persistence means finding a method that works and not stopping until you do. If one approach does not work for you, be prepared to find one that does and adopt it. You are not *abandoning* the goal, but merely changing the *way* in which you go about reaching it. In the example of the work promotion, what are the factors the company considers when assessing your eligibility for promotion? Find out what these criterions are, and work towards them. The point is to invest your time, effort and resources into what is effective, and takes you in the direction you *want* to go. Dogged unthinking persistence alone will not get you anywhere.

As you acquire more and more experience, you will be become better at assessing the situations where change is warranted, and where it pays to persist.

At this point, we have considered the four primary principles. In the next chapter, I will introduce the four attitudes and skills that you should adopt to ensure a more effective and efficient the **application** of the primary principles.

PART 5

The Finishing Touches

Putting all the pieces together

While we attribute many names and description to the qualities needed to succeed, they generally fit into three main categories, namely:

- qualities that start us moving;
- those that keep us moving; and
- that which moves us in the <u>right direction</u> and <u>effectively</u>.

All three categories must be present for our efforts to be effective. It's a given that the first two categories of qualities are necessary as they form the locomotive that drives the train. And I believe that we, as diligent and hard-working people, have what it takes in the first two categories. Yet unless we develop the third category of qualities, we spend too much time and resources in order to reach our goals. If you have begun applying the four principles in your daily life, you should hopefully be experiencing a higher rate of success. However you might feel that:

- the rate of success could be even <u>higher</u> as, at times, you might feel like that you're driving a uncontrollable locomotive that's not always heading in the direction that you want. At times the locomotive feels like it's just spinning its wheels and hardly making any progress at all;

- the results (or the quality and experience of these results) are different from what you expected;
- you frequently encounter delays, obstructions and diversions along the way and you wish that the process could be smoother and quicker.
- you experience inconsistent result even though you may be doing the same things; and you don't know why you succeed on some occasions and fail in the others;
- you feel ill-equipped to adapt whenever you encounter something out of the ordinary.

These are but a few symptoms indicating that the qualities in the third category are missing. The symptoms are numerous and the ways in which they manifest in our lives are myriad. I have cited only a few examples; however upon self-reflection, you will see realise how the absence of any of these attitudes and skills will far-reaching the consequences

In this final chapter, I will touch on the four attitudes and skills that come within the third category, namely

- Understanding;
- Focus;
- Awareness; and
- Practice.

I will refer to them collectively as the four elements. I will show how these four elements supplement the four principles and make us more effective and efficient in what we do. I have referred to each of these four elements throughout the earlier chapters, however as they play very crucial roles in the process of self-improvement, it is necessary to consider them individually.

The first three elements of understanding, focus and awareness can be applied both at a macro (big picture) level as well as at a micro (day-to-day) level. By macro level I am referring to, for example, how we are doing in life as a whole, what our primary goals are. In the context of this chapter, micro level refers to, for example, how we deal with daily life situations, make decisions and interact with others. Practice, on the hand, is something we do in the present moment to everything that is a repetitive activity.

Other than practice, each of the elements are all about how we use of our mind; which means that they can be adopted and applied easily. However understanding and mastering all three elements will require consistent practice and self-reflection. As you begin to consciously apply the elements, you will realise that although they can be applied individually, in many situations these elements complement one another.

Understanding

"Clarity: the state or quality of being clear, distinct and easily perceived or understood." - The Oxford English Dictionary.

If the essence of understanding has to be summarised into one word, it would be "clarity". For the purposes of this chapter, we are considering clarity in the context of thought, purpose, and communication. In short, it's being clear:

- about what we really want;
- on what needs to be done, and the various elements (who, what, where, how) of the action to be taken;
- when communicating to both ourselves and to others what we want and our expectations are; and
- about what others want and what their expectations are when they are communicating with us.

Having a firm understanding is akin to having a firm foundation upon which we build on. The less we understand, the shakier the foundation.

In the "Goals" chapter, we dealt extensively on the need to understand the reasons that resonate with us experientially. We have seen, at a macro level, that when we understand that reason, we are able to generate stronger determination and commitment than if we are unclear about why we set a certain goal in the first place.

It is entirely possible for there to be multiple goals to meet the same primary reason. However by coming from a position of understanding we are able to select the most suitable goal that best serves that reason. It also enables us to map out the processes, milestones and deadlines. Once we have a clear understanding of what we need to do and how to do it, we spend less time ruminating over "what if's" scenarios. The process of decision-making is faster and less complicated. With the clarity that understanding brings, the primary reason becomes both a signpost and the anchor to help us stay the course. When the going gets tough, this primary reason will remind us why we need to keep going. However this is just one aspect of understanding.

At the micro (or application) level, having a firm understanding of the way that we are doing things ensures that our intended course of action is firstly, the best approach under the circumstances and secondly, we are doing it correctly. To achieve this stage of understanding, it is vital not to accept all that we learn at face value. When we blindly accept and apply any process with the naive belief that it will always work, and there's a change of circumstance causing the process to stop working, we become confused. We don't know why we failed even though we followed the process to the letter. We may become doubtful and fearful on how best to proceed.

We encounter problems as a result of lack of understanding when:

- we are unclear about what we or others really want;
- we don't communicate effectively to ourselves or to others;
- we fail to grasp what others are trying to tell us;
- we lack the necessary information, we make assumptions without taking the effort to seek clarification. For instance, we might assume that we know what others want and expect. And we might assume that others know what we want and expect;
- we apply what we learn blindly without grasping the reasons behind what we are doing, or the mechanics of the process itself; and
- we don't critically analyse what we do.

Here are some pointers that I've found useful:

Clarity of need & wants

- Often times we start taking action with only a fuzzy, incomplete picture of what we are going after. Sometimes we may not even have a picture at all! Develop the ability to express your ideas clearly to yourself. It's the same process we use in goal-setting to discern the primary reason that resonates with us experientially. Reducing your thoughts into writing may help you understand them better. Filter out the noise and distractions and see what is truly on your mind. Having a clear goal gives us a a clear and defined finish line and makes the job of communicating our ideas to others easier too.
- Once you have a clear image of the goal in place, have a clear picture of the ingredients that need to fall into place.

Meaning & Context

- In our communications with others, be aware that the other party may attach a different meaning to a word than what we ourselves may be accustomed to. When we fail to realise this possibility, we risk sending the wrong message to the other party. With the benefit of this awareness, we can use the alternative words to convey the message across clearly and completely.

- Because of this distinction, we may similarly run the risk of misunderstanding the message another person is conveying. Because we subconsciously associate a different meaning to the word that the other person is using, in these situations it may be helpful for you to consciously use a substitute word that you are familiar with to convey the same meaning to yourself.

- Understand the context in which others may use a word. We frequently assume that other people will use a word in the same context as we do. Ostensibly this may seem obvious and logical. However you will be surprised how often others may understand words differently from us, even if such differences may be slight. Use words in the context that the listener understands. If we stubbornly stick to the terminology we are comfortable with, we may end up conveying the wrong message to the listener.

- Understand what are the expectations that flow from what is said or written. Ensure that the other party understands, too. These expectation may concern what needs to be done, by whom, and when. It can also refer to the consequences that flow from what is done. Again it may seem obvious that everyone should have the same expectations of what needs to be done, or what the consequences will be. But it's crucial to realise that our expectations are our interpretation of the situation. We are looking at it from only our perspective.

Expectations differ not just from one person to another, but from one organisation to another, and even from one culture to another.

- From my personal experience, disputes usually are a result of firstly, people having differing understanding of what was communicated and secondly, people having differing expectations of what needs to be done or should happen following from what was communicated. People mistakenly assume that their expectations and understanding are identical. Realising that such differences exist help us become aware of areas of potential mistakes and misunderstanding. Ensure that we don't assume that others understand, or that others are making assumptions either.

- Don't be too shy or afraid to ask. Most of all, don't assume. Especially if you are taking on a new activity for the first time. When we choose to remain silent because we are shy or afraid, or choose to rely on assumptions, we are content to simply remain within our comfort zone.

- Don't adopt an "I know that" mindset. Thinking that we know everything already is a disempowering mindset. The mind comes to the conclusion that there's nothing new to learn and shuts out any attempts by others to teach it anything new or better. Whenever it encounters new information, a closed mind comes to the quick conclusion that it's either wrong, or inferior to what it already knows.

- If you are experiencing a nagging feeling that something is amiss, don't suppress it. It's usually the mind trying to tell you that information in certain areas are lacking. Identify the missing information and learn more.

- When learning a skill or a process, be prepared to ask why things are done the way they are. Take the process apart and understand each step. Ask yourself if this is the best way of doing it. What are the assumptions that the process is premised on? What happens to the process or the results if these assumptions no longer hold true? Why hasn't anyone considered doing it differently?

- Don't be content to apply anything you learn purely by rote as this will only yield lackluster results. If you are only able to perform a task purely out of mindless repetition, and if circumstances deviate from the ordinary, you will get stumped as you are unable to accommodate the change in circumstances. But if you have a thorough understanding of the process, you are able to see the correlation between your actions and the outcome. You are able to tailor the process to achieve your specific purpose and be confident that any changes you implement will work.

Focus- the art of channelling

In the context of this chapter, focus means the act of deliberately channelling attention. Focus comes to play at two levels. Firstly, at a macro level, focus means consciously applying our efforts and resources to creating the right mindset, setting the goals and implementing the processes with the ultimate intention of satisfying our intended objective. What we focus on determines the goals we set, the means by which we reach our goals, as well as the consequences flowing from the goals.

Secondly, at a micro level, it refers to where we direct our conscious attention. The latter is different from awareness in that awareness is a passive state of consciousness, whereas focus is the act of consciously channelling our attention to a specific thought or action. In short, focus asks the question "what do we have our eyes on?".

Macro Level Focus

What we focus on defines our actions and outcome

Let's return to the example of the two students taking up the same academic course. One signs up to get a degree to improve his resumé whereas the other is taking up the course purely out of his love and interest of the subject. The first student is likely to focus on finding the fastest, most straightforward way of completing the course subjects and preparing for the assignments and exams. He is unlikely to stray too far from his course materials. It's only a matter of doing what's absolutely necessary to get his degree.

On the other hand, as the second student is doing it out of his love for the subject, his approach is likely to be different. He may be more thorough in the way he goes about his studies, finding out more about the topics that interest him and conduct research beyond what's required for his course work. He is not interested in just how well he will fare in the final assignment or examination but to have a better grasp of the subject too.

Taking yet another example, let's say there are two companies. One company's primary focus is to provide the best quality of service to its customers, whereas the second company's objective is to make the most profits by incurring the least costs. In order to provide the best possible service to its clients, the first company will not always opt for the cheapest way to do things. It may spare no expense to provide its clients with the best possible experience. On the other hand, the second company may be prepared to compromise the customer experience by incurring only what is absolutely necessary to produce its services.

Discerning a change in focus

At times, we can discern a change in focus is taking place by looking at the change in the way that a company goes about its business For instance, this may occurs when there is a change in a company's management or ownership. The new owners may have a different objective (to maximise profits) than that of the original owners (to give their customers the best experience possible). The new owners will implement changes to the company's policies, employee incentive programs and benchmarks to align them with the new objectives. The change in focus will manifest itself in the quality of the company's products and services.

Unconscious change in focus

When we change the objectives that we are focusing on, how we achieve our goals will change and so will the way that we measure progress. Because of this, when we unknowingly change our focus midway, we may abandon all that we have been doing so far. And we could also end up with a result that satisfies neither the original intention nor the new one! As a result of which, we feel frustrated that we have nothing to show for all our efforts and fail to understand how things turned out this way.

In the first example, the two students ostensibly appear to have a common goal, namely to take up and complete the course. Likewise the two companies in the second example, namely to provide service to their customers. However as each of the students and companies are focusing on different objectives, they all go about studying and doing business in vastly different ways. What we focus on therefore determines how we will work towards our goals, and how we use our time, efforts and resources.

Problems with Focus at a Macro Level

When we fail to grasp the correlation between what we focus on at a "big picture" level and the results we get, we may:

- experience mixed feelings when taking on the project as we don't really feel that it resonates with us experientially;
- spread our time and resources too thinly pursuing too many objectives at once;
- experience inconsistent results;
- become discouraged when we seem to be making too little progress in spite of the effort we put in;
- discover the results after we reach our goal do not satisfy the primary reason at all.

These problems may arise because (i) we don't stay focused on the reasons behind our goals, (ii) we try to find a primary reason to justify our goal only after we've set down the goal, (iii) we don't stay focused on the process by which we are working towards the goal, or (iv) we switch our focus (or become distracted) from the primary reason to something else midway to the goal.

Let's take the example of a person wishing to lose weight. There are many diet and exercise programs out there, depending on what one wishes to achieve. Let's say that he is in the habit of switching from one diet program to another, or from one exercise regime to another without any intention of following through with any of them. He will only stay on one program until another program comes along that catches his eye. As a result, he would have invested a lot of time and effort without much to show for it.

Micro Level Focus

At a micro level, failing to appreciate the significance of this mental trait means that we will experience results that vary from one day to another, as they will reflect the level of attention that we place on our actions on any given day.

We may lose focus at a micro level when:

- we become distracted by too much "noise" and options that clamour for our attention. These distractions may be caused by ourselves, other people or circumstances;
- we might become distracted by other demands on our time and resources. These demands could be those that are related to the goal itself or other areas of our life;
- there is a lack of certainty in what we need to focus on. This uncertainty may be caused by not understanding our goal or what needs to be done. Uncertainty may also arise in situations where we need to work with others, and there is a failure to arrive at a common consensus on how to approach a goal;
- we are emotionally affected when we encounter obstacles, setbacks and failure;
- we are overwhelmed by the enormity of what we have to do. Just as when we encounter the Wall, everything seems insurmountable;
- we allow ourselves to act in a state of automatism. We aren't present in the act itself. In this situation, we not only lack focus, we don't have a sense of awareness either;
- we are simply physically tired or mentally fatigued; or
- we crave a change simply for the sake of change, especially when the feeling of staleness sets in.

Lack of focus impacts the direction as well as the pace of our progress. This will manifest itself in the following ways:

- we experience a perpetual sense of uncertainty, of what we are doing, where we are going and whether we are making any progress at all;

- we experience inconsistent results, depending on the level of our focus on any given day. This is significant in performance-related activities such as sports where winning or losing depends on us being present and focusing our attention on what really matters;
- we might encounter confusion, and the whole project comes to a stall. We frequently see this happening when it is a group effort;
- we waste time and resources starting one project, abandoning it, and starting on another one;
- overall morale and confidence drops as we aren't sure what we are focusing on. When we are unsure, whether from a lack of understanding or focus, we are unprepared to commit our full efforts into the venture.

All things at its proper time and place

Have you had moments when you're at the office amidst piles of work and you're thinking that you should be spending more time with the family. You become distracted. Your mind just isn't in what's before you and it shows up in the quality of your work.

And when you are with your family, you're not experiencing the quality time that you crave. Quite ironically your mind may drift off to the work related matters. You would be checking your phone for incoming emails or text messages from co-workers. You aren't paying attention to what your children and spouse are saying. You hear their voices but you aren't really listening. You go through the motions, and your family members are aware that whilst you're physically present, your mind is far far away.

Why does this happen? It's a result of not being present to the task at hand. Consequently the mind pre-occupies itself by thinking about **other** tasks or problems when you can't really do anything about it at that very moment. This becomes a distraction that causes unhappiness and dissatisfaction. Make a conscious therefore to focus solely on the task before you. Whenever a thought pops up that interferes with your work or quality time with the family, refocus again to what you are doing at the very moment. Don't remonstrate yourself if you don't succeed in the beginning, just persist at it. By bringing your consciousness to just what is before you now, you become more effective at work and are able to truly enjoy your time with your family or your pastime.

Regaining focus:

- Remember what was truly important to you. Look back at the primary reason behind the goal. Re-kindle the buzz and excitement that got us started in the venture in the very first place.
- Have a firm understanding of what the goal is. You can't achieve a target that you don't have. Make the commitment to stick to the process, milestones and deadlines.
- Practise a constant sense of awareness (which we will discuss further later on) of our thoughts as well as our actions. A strong sense of awareness creates a self-discipline to constantly re-align our thoughts and actions to our purpose, just as a ship navigates through a stormy sea.
- Don't make changes in important projects, simply for the sake of trying something different. If the change serves no purpose, do not pursue it.

- Take the effort to consciously assess the available options, and then decide. Be less easily persuaded by what others may say or suggest. We live in an environment that constantly inundates us with distractions. Learn to filter out the unnecessary and be confident enough to re-commit to what you're doing. Often changing for the sake of change itself will yield different results. Different doesn't necessarily mean better. But choosing a new approach involves abandoning all the progress we have made in favour of starting from ground zero again. Consequently more time and resources are spent on the venture.

- Rest when necessary. We need to recharge both the mind and body to continue to do our best work. We often belabour under the mistaken belief that we need to push on in spite of our fatigue. However when we are well-rested, we have a sharper mind and a body that's functioning optimally.

- Sometimes staying focus at the micro level is simply just about putting one foot in front of the other in spite of everything that is in our way. It's about focusing on what's immediately before us, completing that and going on to the next task. It may seem that we are making scant progress. However it's when we look back later on that we come to realise we have travelled a great distance.

- Practise staying focused. As with many other things, the more we practise, the better we get at it. Just as physical exercise increases our body's ability to lift heavier and run further, persistent practice increases our mental stamina thereby allowing us to us to remain aware of our thoughts and actions for longer periods of time.

- Realise that what we are feeling whenever we encounter obstacles and temporary failure does not necessarily mean that problem lies with the goal or the process. We should not change course *in reaction* to our emotions. Rather we need to understand why we are feeling the way we do, and it's usually just a mental interpretation of what's happening. And when we carry out an objective assessment of that mental interpretation, we discover that it has nothing to do with the goal itself or the process.

Focusing at a micro level

Take a simple chore, such as brushing your teeth. See if you can keep your mind focused solely on the act of brushing throughout the entire process. You may realise that your mind will wander to at least half a dozen different things before you finish. Don't be daunted. Persist. Be conscious of your actions and the physical sensations. How the toothbrush feels in your hands and the feeling of the bristles brushing against your gums, the insides of your mouth, and along the teeth. Be in the here and now.

Progress from this to more complex but routine activities. The idea is to see how long you can maintain your thought flows in the present moment. And to lose the 'self' into the activity. That's when your full abilities and mental faculties are fully focused at the task at hand.

Awareness

We learn life's lessons only when fully awake and truly present.

"Awareness" is defined in the Oxford English Dictionary as having knowledge or perception of a situation or a fact. In the context of our discussion, awareness can be described as presence. Being here now. It refers to the moment-by-moment consciousness of our thoughts, emotions, action as well as our surroundings. We frequently exist in a state of foggy-mindedness, allowing most of our actions to be dictated purely by our habits and in reaction to external circumstances and stimuli. Awareness opens up our minds to the existence of choices and our innate ability to take deliberate action. Awareness works closely with focus to channel our efforts and resource to best achieve what we set out to do. If focus is like a beam of light that pierces the darkness, awareness is the ability to discern the objects that the beam of light reveals.

Why "awareness" and not "mindfulness"?

Because the term "mindfulness" suggests only mental attentiveness. However in the context of this topic, "awareness" encompasses mental and emotional attentiveness, engaging all our five primary senses and the entire body itself.

Awareness may seem, at first glance, to be something that we practice only at a day-to-day or moment-by-moment level. However awareness plays a role at a macro level, too. Macro level awareness refers to the ability to have a bird's eye view of our life's landscape. For instance, it enables us to see how our beliefs have an influence on our lives as a whole. Without this ability, we may not see the correlation between our limiting beliefs and the quality of our lives.

Awareness enables us to discern the four root causes of the problems that we might face. Without it, life situations will just appear as disparate, unrelated events that we address on an ad hoc basis rather than holistically. We fail to see the woods for the trees. With awareness we are able to perceive the consequences of any changes we make as well as measure our progress.

Awareness enables us to constantly improve ourselves by allowing our day-to-day action and major life decisions to influence one another. How? Initially our "big picture" decisions will determine the course of our day-to-day actions. As we go about our day-to-day activities, our awareness the micro level enables us to see ways in which we can improve the way we do things. We begin fine-tuning and improving. We may even begin to see alternative macro level decisions that weren't obvious in the beginning. This then starts the process of discovery all over again. I will elaborate on how awareness plays a role in each principle, and its relevance will become more apparent.

Beliefs

At the macro level, beyond just understanding that we become what we think about, awareness is necessary to help us see that we have limiting beliefs and attitudes, and what they are. If we are unaware of these limitations, we will habitually continue to have the same limiting mindset that hold us back from true change. Having identified these limitations, we can adopt a more positive set of beliefs. At this stage, having a keen sense of awareness helps us take notice whenever our mind tries to revert to its old ways of thinking. Moment-by-moment awareness creates continuous opportunities for us to make small, incremental (literally) second-by-second choices of how we think and the attitude we maintain in the life situations that we encounter. Practicing moment-by-moment awareness is great because even when we momentarily drop our guard, and made one decision based on our old beliefs, we can immediately pick ourselves up and make the very next decision based on our new set of beliefs!

We can mentally prepare ourselves for life situations that we can anticipate. In these situations, we pay close attention to our train of thoughts and remind ourselves not to slip into our old way of thinking the moment we encounter a difficulty. With consistent practice, we soon realise that we can maintain an awareness of our mindset even in situations where we can't prepare ourselves beforehand. We become proficient in observing that we are about to lapse into a negative way of thinking, stop it, and consciously choose to keep a positive mindset instead. As the new sets of beliefs and thought processes become firmly established, we will see how the micro level changes improve the quality of our lives, our relationships, our work and how we perceive the world.

Goal setting

Awareness plays a vital role when we address the question "why". It requires soul-searching to comprehend the reason that truly resonates with us at the sensorial, emotional and experiential level. What is it that moves us whenever we think about the objective that we are seeking to achieve? What is the "feedback" that we get from it?

Once we have established that compelling primary reason, we have to be aware that there may be several ways in which that "why" may be answered. In fact, we might even realise that the goal we originally set out to achieve may not be the most effective way of addressing these reasons.

With awareness we filter through all the various options before we settle down on the few main goals. Once the goal is established, we can define the milestones and ingredients that will get us there. At this juncture, awareness comes into the picture again. For instance, in relation to the information needed for the project, it allows us to determine what we know, and what we don't. And we can use that as the starting point of our information gathering process. And as we go along, we need to maintain an awareness of both the small issues that crop up, as well as bird's eye perspective to ensure that we are heading in the right direction. It's only when we are present and aware, we discover opportunities for change and improvement.

Action

On a broader scale, awareness has a role in everything that we do physically. However it's just that we act like automatons 70% to 80% of the time. We might go through an entire day acting purely out of habit without being conscious of it. And we wonder how a whole day could go by, and we didn't even feel engaged! How easy it is then to live an un-lived life! Yes, it takes considerable effort and concentration to be able to stay tuned for long periods of time. Yet this is necessary to ensure our life journey stays true to the charted course. This is especially so during moments when attention is truly needed in the details. Glossing over these ostensibly minor details results in a much lower quality outcome.

Being present

By "presence", I am referring to being conscious of where we are and what we are doing right now. Often we live our lives on auto-pilot. We are present physically but our minds may be far away, jumping from one thought to another. Is it any surprise we feel like we are living in a dream? Therefore our challenge is to overcome the habitual tendency to slip into this "auto-pilot" state.

When you are engaged in an activity, for example, if you are writing, be present in the act of the writing itself, and the emotions you feel. Be in the moment when you choose the words you write, so that you accurately relay your intended meaning. This is when being conscious of what you are thinking about is important. Don't let the mind drift on its own to events that are irrelevant and unrelated to the task at hand. Another example where such an experience of presence can be felt is when we are listening to music. When we are truly present in the act of listening, we can "feel" the emotions that the composer is expressing through his music. We try to hear and capture the little nuances, instead of fogging out the details.

Here are some of my personal observations when practising awareness in my life. I hope that they will serve as pointers to you:

- Resist the mind's attempts to think about the future or the past. It is only in the present that we can realistically accomplish what we set out to do. While we can certainly make plans for the future, but they are always implemented in the present.
- Cultivate a state of mind of thinking only when it's necessary. There is an appropriate time and place for thinking and planning. This may sound ridiculous at first blush. But

remember: we are *not* our mind. We should direct our mind to do our bidding, and not the other way around. After all, if you think about it, we don't allow our limbs to flail about continuously and uncontrollably. They only move to do our bidding, when they are called upon perform a specific act. So why should the mind be any different? Thinking has its role, but it cannot become an all-encompassing activity. Try walking around without a single thought in your head. It feels liberating!

Silencing the mind

The picture becomes much clearer when we choose not to be distracted by the "noise" within and without. We put our complete attention to task that is before us without shifting our thoughts unnecessarily to the past or the future. Just remain here and now. In this silence, answers will come to us. Perhaps the answers were always there, hidden behind the doubts and worry that always preoccupy our mind. Focus and awareness allows these thoughts and ideas to surface slowly to our consciousness, like air bubbles floating up to the surface of a still lake.

- The mind loves creating "what-if" scenarios in which it can play out various outcomes. At times it even creates imaginary worlds within which it can take up "residence". Such activities are only a source of distraction and negativity if the mind reinforces low self-esteem or limiting beliefs in the make-believe world. Whenever you catch yourself playing out "what-if" scenarios, stop the thought process and bring yourself back to the present moment.
- Be aware of what's happening inside you. Don't analyse the thoughts and emotions and feelings, as this will just give the chattering mind an opportunity to go off on a tangent, but just be aware. Then bring the mind back to stillness.

- However it's important to realise that being the observer "observing" the thought process is *not* the end goal. There is no point in continuously observing the thoughts, as this means that thoughts are *still* occurring. This would be self-defeating.

- Ultimately our end goal is to be conscious of only the act and to do the act with the absence of additional thought or unnecessary mental activity. However the intermediate stage of observing the thought is necessary, as otherwise we will not be conscious that we are in fact (1) doing it (thinking) and (2) become part of the thought process. As a result of which, we have become separated from that which we are supposed to be doing or experiencing. Both the extraneous thoughts and "observer" state disappears.

- Observe your emotions too. Don't interpret them, but just be aware of them. Our emotions are usually not the issue. Rather it is the **thoughts** that we have about these emotions that are the source of our troubles. Without this additional baggage, our emotions would just come and go. However the ensuing thoughts cause them to outstay their welcome and outlive their purpose.

Choice

As mentioned earlier, awareness comprises of two aspects. One aspect refers to being conscious of the many choices we face every single day, and being able to deliberately choose one over another. The second aspect is the awareness that there are consequences to the choices we make. Lacking a sense of awareness at both levels causes us not understand why we are in the the predicament we find ourselves in or the stroke of good fortune that we are experiencing. Without the benefit of this understanding, we might conclude that our fate is cast in stone, and runs on a preordained course and cannot be changed.

Actually the road to success is chartered and traversed moment-by-moment. Little, if any, is ever left to run automatically. Consider this: if success could be attained simply by sleepwalking through life, then why don't we experience success more frequently? It's taking all those infinitesimally small effort, time and again, that the others habitually overlook, or are too tired or (more likely) too lazy to do that makes all the difference. It might not be much, but it still needs to be done.

Success is seldom a case of accomplishing a single task which requires one titanic effort. Instead success frequently entails diligently completing numerous small tasks that require but a small amount of effort each. Most of us would very much prefer the former as it's a one-off affair. Besides, it makes for a more interesting personal story, too.

Because of this attitude, we tend to put off making these small decisions and putting them off to another day because we're too tired, not in the mood or put them on the back-burner in favour of more "urgent" priorities. On the other hand, people who achieve notable success constantly make these decisions and act on them regardless of how busy or tired they may be. In doing so, they gradually widen the gap that separates them from the others.

Success is not just a matter of saying "yes" to just the big decisions, it's also making the right decision hundreds (if not thousands) of times to all the small but equally important issues every day. On some days, the "yes" decision comes easily and with conviction. On others, our decision to say "yes" comes with doubt and hesitation. That's perfectly fine, as it means we are still on course. We can't win them all decisively. One some days we will make it just by the skin of our teeth. These are actually the hard-won victories. Savour them. On some days we may even cave in despite our best efforts. We might even have done it intentionally! During these times, don't be too hard on yourself. All is not lost. It's not a case of all-or-nothing. We just pick ourselves up and continue walking.

Problem solving

Awareness allows us to discern the different problems we are facing, whether in the form of a wall, plateau, pile-up or vicious cycle. Until we are able to define the problem, all attempts at solving it will be largely hit and miss affair. To be effective, we need to stay focused on our end goal, i.e. what needs to be accomplished at the end of the day, and how that problem is keeping us from attaining that end state. Without this discernment, we would be doomed to repeatedly do what we have always done and not understanding why the same problems keep cropping up. With an acute sense of awareness comes the ability to express the problem clearly and objectively, without any uncertainty or foggy thinking, and identify the solutions to overcome them. Through constant practice, our ability to identify problems and solutions become faster. Issues that may take others weeks, months or even a lifetime to resolve will be solved in a fraction of that time.

> <u>This is the last thing I will do…</u>
>
> The thing is, we spend a majority of our conscious lives dwelling in our thoughts rather than the active participatory world. Even when we are doing something, we aren't present in the activity, but in the <u>thoughts</u> about the activity! It's not unusual for the mind to be even thinking about a myriad other things. So are we really there? One method I use to bring myself back to the present is to play a game I call "This is the last time I … today.". It's a variation of the motto "Live today like it's your last". Even if we are aware of how fragile life truly is, yet somehow the latter just doesn't give us the much needed sense of immediacy. We always think that tomorrow will inevitably come.

This variation on the motto imparts a more immediate sense of finality. This is how it works. Whenever I am doing something, I remind myself that this is the last time that I'm doing that activity for the day. For instance, if I'm eating my breakfast in the morning, I remind myself that this is the last time I'm eating my breakfast for that day. This event will never occur again in my life. I immediately snap back to the present moment and become more aware of my actions, and the sensations that I am feeling. I feel more alive. The food tastes better. The experiences become sharper, clearer and more enjoyable.

Inner conversations

"Change" suggests trying some thing that is not within our normal scheme of things. The very first opponent to change - of whatever nature - is ourselves. Internal "conversations" will take place between the mind (the logical) and the heart (the emotional) on the merits of the change. They may be over how the changes will affect our lives, our routines, the amount of energy or effort needed to make it work, the time it will take, or even how they will affect our relationship with the people around us.

Because this internal conversation takes place so frequently that it has become second nature to us, the important thing is to notice that this "conversation" is even taking place! Whenever you are aware this "conversation" is taking place, consciously stop this train of thought and believe in the greater good that the change will bring. Focus on the positive experience that you will feel.

For instance, if you're focusing on weight loss, imagine how light and agile you would feel. Feel the happiness of looking good, and being able to do more with the additional energy and drive.

The inner voice that is urging you to give up can, at times, be very seductive especially when your willpower is low, you're facing obstacles or you've hit a plateau. It is at such times that the mind deludes you into thinking that there is no more improvement, things are not working out, and it's better to just give up. It is crucial to catch yourself as these negative thoughts are taking place. Disrupt it, and calm your mind down. Allow your emotions to re-emphasise the benefits of the change.

Bring your mind back to the now, and to the task at hand. Take the task through, step-by-step. Continue to be in the present and focusing on the task. In time, the mind will stop fighting back, and you will have overcome the resistance for now. Certain routines (such as an exercise program) almost always feels uncomfortable, even unpleasant, before you start. But this discomfort always goes away once you're doing it. It's been said that it takes about 6 months for a new habit or routine to form. So take heart that there is light at the end of the tunnel. Once you're past the 6-month threshold, the new routine would become a part of you!

Making change possible through awareness

A common problem is that we don't make a conscious effort to analyse what went wrong. Once we encounter the same failure or bad experience, we banish it to the furthest corner of our mind. We sulk, get angry, or feel sorry for ourselves. Until the next cycle of failure and frustration.

Hence the first step out of this rut is to understand what is it that we keep doing that is wrong. This is where we adopt the state of conscious awareness. By "conscious" awareness, I mean that we have to be mentally "present" when the mistake is made. Or if that moment is not immediately apparent, by virtue that we are "present" throughout the process, we have a better recollection of what had happened. Once we isolate the elements that require improvement, we introduce new changes to the process and see how well it works.

Integrating the changes, and observing the outcome is the second phase at which we commonly encounter problems. Oftentimes we don't consciously try to implement the changes. And we allow ourselves to lapse into our old habitual way of doing things. Or we may be overwhelmed by a life situation when it happens and, despite our better judgment, we relapse to our tried and true methods which, of course, lead to the same results. We can only overcome our old habits by being conscious at the moment when the cue appears which prompt the old familiar routines. We take deliberate steps not to do what we are accustomed to doing, regardless of our fear of failure, what others may say, or how uncomfortable the change may feel.

Practice

> "Any idiot can face a crisis - it's day to day living that wears you out." - Anton Chekov

It's my belief that we encounter truly monumental obstacles that break our resolve very infrequently. A substantial part of our lives are comprised of life situations that occur over and over again. And it is actually the day-to-day drudgery and grind that hold us back from making any real progress towards our life goals. The good news is that we can apply practice to our daily lives to improve the way we do things. With practice comes proficiency, effectiveness and efficiency in what we do.

Practice plays an especially important role when we embark on something new, whether it's a change in our attitude, belief system, goal-setting, or putting our plans into action. This is not to say that practice ceases to be important later on, but it's at its nascent stage that consistent, persistent and conscious practice lays down a solid, reliable foundation for everything that follows thereafter.

"Practice" is a word we frequently associate with the realm of sports and music. Images of athletes and musicians performing one aspect of the game or a musical piece over and of again comes to mind. However practice does not take place only in these situations. For our purposes, practice can be described as a process of progressive improvement through repetition. Viewed in this way, practice no longer becomes the exclusive domain of athletes and musicians. Practice can take place in our daily lives. While we can practice or rehearse certain aspects of our lives in the same way that musicians do, however most of our life routines cannot be rehearsed in this fashion. There are just too many "moving parts" to recreate. Furthermore how many of us really have the luxury of time to practice this way?

Everyday life as a venue of practice

Every day we encounter life situations that we can use as "practice sessions" to apply our new belief systems, attitudes, and habits. These opportunities are always present. But if we don't see them from this perspective, we can't take advantage of them; and unlike a controlled classroom environment, you will find that the practice sessions are harder on some days than others.

Nonetheless in the same way that practice in a controlled environment allows us to spot areas where our performance is lacking, we can also analyse real life practice in the same way, too. Actively review and assess your performance to determine the areas that need improvement. And you will often find that there are. This is not an exercise in self-criticism, but our focus is to become better. Unless we improve the way we respond to these life situations, we will experience the same results whenever we encounter a similar situation in the future.

> Success is not a consequence of the act of practice alone, rather it comes from what happens **during** the practice. What we are striving for is quality rather than purely quantity.

Reaping the full rewards of practice

For the purposes of this chapter, we are not looking at the act of practising per se, but the mindset of practice. What are our attitudes and beliefs towards practice? How do we feel about it? What are the the mental images that practice conjures up? Are the images of progressive improvement, taking you closer to your goals, or are the images of an activity that is dull, repetitive and yields little return? Having the right perception helps us approach practice differently; with purpose, energy, and enthusiasm. It then becomes an essential process by which we become progressively better and better at what we do. And that's what practice is all about. Here are some consequences of unconscious and unfocused practice:

- the results don't justify the amount of "practice" put in, because what is being done does not effectively address the our weaknesses;
- we use more time and energy and resources than is necessary. As a result of this inefficient use of resources, we draw on our resources that are intended for other activities. This in turn affects our performance in these activities;
- we experience an overall delay in the progress towards our goal. We are ostensibly doing all the right things, but it's as if we are hitting a glass wall. In extreme cases, we encounter performance plateaus;
- we experience spotty, inconsistent results;
- we feel disillusioned when we don't reach our goal. We may come to the wrong conclusion that we "just aren't good in this";
- we also experience frustration, unhappiness and confusion over the lack of progress.

Here are some possible causes:

- the thought of practice invokes negative images and connotations;
- we misunderstand the concept of practice. We may believe that so long as we put in the time and make the numbers, that's all that needs to be done;
- as a result of the two points above, we just go through the motions and not really "in" it. As soon as the practice session begins we lapse into a state of automatism and act purely out of force of habit. And because we aren't focused on what we are doing, we get easily distracted by our thoughts and our surroundings;
- we go into a practice session without specific goals and objectives to improve the areas that need improvement, or we may not have any idea how the individual sessions will complement each other to achieve the overall goal. Consequently we go into practice sessions aimlessly, believing that we just need to "give it time" and we will improve;
- we fail to analyse the way we practice to ensure that it's the most effective and efficient way of doing things;
- we practice only what we are already good at, and avoid the areas that truly need our attention; or
- we emulate the practice routines of others without realising that our weaknesses may be different.

It's not that you're doing it but <u>how</u> you're doing it that makes the difference. Here are some considerations:

- "Practice" might be a word that you associate with unpleasant memories. Of piano classes, ballet lessons or sports that were imposed on you by your parents, when you would rather be doing something else altogether. As such practice feels like it's best left in the past. Remember that this is a mental construct. We <u>can</u> choose to attribute anything with "good" or "bad" qualities. Look at practice with a new perspective; as a vital tool to success. After all, we didn't begin walking in our very first attempt. Why then do we assume that we can achieve anything more complex than that without practise?

- Strive for quality over over quantity. If you focus on quality, you may discover that you don't need to practise that frequently;

- The purpose of practice is to firstly, improve the areas that we are weak in and secondly, to improve our overall performance. With that in mind, it's necessary to set an end goal and sub-goals. Sub-goals become the goals for the individual practice sessions. In this way, our practice sessions will have both purpose and direction. And as a whole, all our practice sessions will collectively advance us towards the end goal.

- Don't treat practice are something you "have to do". Don't just go through the motions, or you will miss the whole point of practice. Do it with all your enthusiasm and don't spare any effort. Half-baked efforts only create a muscle memory of mediocrity.

- When we are in the company of others, we often unconsciously adopt the mindset and physiology of the people around us when we practice. Naturally if they are just going through the motions, we may unconsciously do the same thing, too. But you don't have to. You can, and should, put yourself into every practice session in order to reap the most benefit out of it.

- When you practice, make an effort to engage all your senses and your whole being (physically, mentally and emotionally) so that you become fully immersed in the activity. You are no longer just performing the activity but become one with it.

- Learn, be aware and improve. Otherwise our sphere of expertise will remain the same size and practice ends up being an exercise of reinforcing existing bad habits and processes.
- Use "proper form". This term is used in sports, particularly weight training, to describe adopting the proper stance, body movements and process when executing an exercise using heavy weights. Proper form is necessary to reap the full benefits of exercise and to minimise injuries. Using proper form in all other types of activities enables us to reap the full benefits of the activity in question, as well as to perform at our best in that moment. What this means is that we have to commit our fullest attention, focus and presence of mind to the activity before us. We perform with full mental attentiveness, using the correct method and processes. Allowing our mind to drift assures us that our energies and efforts are not all channelled to the work at hand. Secondly, lack of proper form increases the likelihood of mistakes. That in turn necessitate us spending more time, energy and resources repeating the process! Better then to avoid doing it rather than exhausting our energy and resources performing lackadaisically.

CLOSING

So those are the four elements that complement the four primary principles.

It is my sincere hope that you will not just read this book passively and it has inspired thought and, more importantly, action. If you have come so far, you have already invested a considerable amount of time. So reap the rewards of that investment by putting what you have learnt into action. If what you've been doing so far has not brought you success, then what have you to lose in trying something new? Don't hesitate. Don't put it off till tomorrow. Don't let other people or circumstances dictate the types and quality of your life experiences.

I hope that you are convinced now that nothing is truly set in stone. You **do** hold your destiny in your own hands. You create the story of your life. Granted that we can't control all that happens in our lives, but we can control how we interpret and respond. You are an active participant of your life and the world that you live in. Success can be visualised, planned and progressively worked on, whether they are small goals, big ones or the truly great ones. Nothing is left to chance. This alone allows your life story to be an empowering and inspiring one.

As I said in the beginning, what this book can do for you depends on how much time and effort you're prepared to invest in putting the four principles into practice and making them a part of your daily life. I therefore urge you to them at the earliest possible opportunity if you haven't already done so. In particular, the first principle is the easiest to start with since it merely involves a change in the state of mind. The change begins from the inside and manifests itself outwards, and not the other way around.

Hopefully what has been covered in this book prompts you to reflect and see the correlation between what your present attitudes, and way of doing things have influenced your life experience thus far. May it inspire you to pluck up the courage and determination to change your current mindset and see its effect. I hope that by creating new mindsets you have a new way of looking at yourself, the people and the world around you.

So where do I go from here, you may ask. The principles are essentially tools. You are ultimately left with these questions that only you can answer:

- what's important to *you*, and will bring meaning to your life. In short, what do you say to yourself what your life's about?
- what *your* goals will be. What are the underlying reasons that have experiential resonance with you;

- what needs to be done in order to achieve them, and the best way to achieve them given your personal circumstances.

With persistent searching your life goals will ultimately reveal themselves. This may not happen immediately. And definitely they won't reveal themselves all at once! Just as life never remains static, the things that resonate with us experientially do not remain the same throughout our lives. In time you may even discover that your life goals will change as you mature and as you take on more responsibilities. What was important to you when you were a child ceases to be so when you are a teenager. What may have been important to you as a teenager ceases to significant when you become an adult. And so on. When this happens, you'd just need to repeat the process of self-discovery again, understand what resonates with you then, and set new goals accordingly.

Secondly, I hope that you are inspired to read more books on self-improvement. Many books have been written about them, examining each element in great detail. I encourage you to read them to gain a deeper understanding. This should not, by any means, be the one and only book that you read on this subject matter. I hope that what had prompted you to pick this book up will keep you on the course of self-discovery. Many great books have been written that go in-depth into the many topics that we have touched on, such as time management, goal setting, human relationships and so on. I strongly encourage you to read them. The time spent will be well invested. With each book, you will gain nuggets of new ideas and insights that may just give you novel ideas or reveal a new perspective. The key to continuous personal growth is a commitment to continuous learning. The day we are convinced that we can stop learning is the day that we stop growing.

Lastly, I hope that you will teach others how to "fish" by imparting and sharing the invaluable gift of knowledge and experience so that they, too, can benefit from what you have learnt in your life journey. Share them. Also share what worked for you, and help others overcome their obstacles and challenges. Write them down in *your* book. Show the people you come into contact of the possibilities that await us, if we but only take the effort to direct our thoughts and actions. Live your life as a positive example and inspiration to others. Together we can all collectively create an awareness that it is indeed possible to live the life of our dreams by understanding and applying the primary principles. May you experience life as a truly wonderful and exciting journey. I wish you all the very best of luck. God bless you.